NO ONE EVER TOLD US THAT

NO ONE EVER TOLD US THAT

*Money and Life Lessons
for Young Adults*

JOHN D. SPOONER

WILEY

Published by John Wiley & Sons, Inc., Hoboken, New Jersey.
Published simultaneously in Canada.

For general information on our other products and services or for technical support, please contact our Customer Care Department within the United States at (800) 762–2974, outside the United States at (317) 572–3993 or fax (317) 572–4002.

Wiley publishes in a variety of print and electronic formats and by print-on-demand. Some material included with standard print versions of this book may not be included in e-books or in print-on-demand. If this book refers to media such as a CD or DVD that is not included in the version you purchased, you may download this material at http://booksupport.wiley.com. For more information about Wiley products, visit www.wiley.com.

Library of Congress Cataloging-in-Publication Data:

Spooner, John D.
  No one ever told us that : money and life lessons for young adults / John D. Spooner.
    pages cm
  Includes index.
  ISBN 978-1-118-99223-4 (cloth); ISBN 978-1-118-99226-5 (ePDF);
  ISBN 978-1-118-99224-1 (ePub)
  1. Investments–Miscellanea.   2. Finance, Personal–Miscellanea.   3. Conduct of life–Miscellanea.   I. Title.
  HG4521.S7184 2015
  332.024–dc23   2015007712

Printed in the United States of America

10 9 8 7 6 5 4 3 2 1

DISCLAIMER

I am a writer. But I also happen to run a wealth management business under the umbrella of a major investment banking firm. These dual careers are distinctly separate from one another. This right brain, left brain life seems to work fine for me.

But my opinions expressed within these chapters are strictly from my own experiences, and are my own observations.

John D. Spooner

For my clients and special friends who have taught me all the lessons.
And for my sister Susie, for so many reasons.

CONTENTS

PART II   BECOMING FINANCIALLY SECURE

PART III BECOMING YOUR OWN PERSON

ACKNOWLEDGMENTS

In no special order, my thanks to the following people for their help in bringing this advice to their young adults who need gentle shoves in the right directions.

Even if my helpers didn't realize at the time how much they added to my writing of the book, they made it possible: Weld Henshaw, Bob and Debbie First, Robert Sprung, Yvonne Russell, Alan Miller, Mike Sandler, Fred Greenman, Bill and Judy Cowin, Dr. Stuart Mushlin, Jeff Levine, Andy Hunter, Bill Eisen, Joe Rooney, Suzanne DelVecchio, and Nat Bickford.

And all the caring people at John Wiley & Sons.

Above all, agent and friend, John Taylor "Ike" Williams, and his associate, Katherine Flynn.

INTRODUCTION

This is a book for all of you *new* grown-ups, out in the world for long enough to have experienced some early bumps in the road, and long enough to know how challenging this new century is for you, in all areas of your still-young lives.

I speak to you as if you are my children, all of them relatively new grown-ups, and needing practical advice for all these new crossroads you face.

I have advised, and still advise, thousands of people, in hundreds of professions and careers. And I've done this for more than 50 years. No rookie, no virgin either, in finding solutions to so many of life's problems.

And as you all are at various new crossroads, I'm at another major one myself.

After my last book, *No One Ever Told Us That,* had been out for several months, a young man knocked on my office door. He seemed to be in his late twenties or early thirties, in a suit and tie, with highly polished English shoes. I seldom see young people so turned out. He was holding a small package wrapped in bright paper, like a birthday present.

"Do you have a minute?" he asked.

"Not really, I said, "but come on in."

He held up the package. "This is for you," he said. "You changed my life."

"How did I do that?" I said. "Although I'm flattered."

"I read your book," he said. "In a chapter about the problems in almost all families there was a line. I've had issues with my family for years and it was eating me up, having to stifle my feelings. Your line was, 'Love your family, but don't let them suck the oxygen out of the room.' I kept thinking about that line. And it gave me the courage to finally speak out. When I did, years hiding these things just fell off my back. Thank you for changing my life."

I opened the present.

"It's pictures done by my favorite artist," he said. "He does graffiti."

I thanked him and asked him to tell me about himself, which he did. And then he said, "You know, you should write a book for us, for me and my friends. We're out of school for 10 years or more, married or not, kids or not, parents who you can tell are going to be needy, and jobs, careers we're not sure about. So many things we're not sure about. We need a lot of help."

This was a young man, suddenly honest about so many things, and not finding many answers, particularly in practical ways. After he left I had a flash about my first years in business, trying to scratch a living as a young stockbroker. My ambition then, in the early 1960s, was to make a six-dollar commission before lunch. My share would be one-third, or two dollars. I figured that two bucks would pay for lunch, and whatever I made in the afternoon would be gravy. Before I had launched in this career, I mentioned to my father that I was considering business school.

"You've been in school long enough," he said. "Time to go to work."

Like the young man knocking on my door, I knew little or nothing about so much. And now I was out in life, a stranger in a strange world, wondering and worrying about almost everything, including: Would anyone ever love me? Would I ever get married?

Now I feel like I'm almost back at those beginnings long ago.

My wife of 45 years, Susan, died of lung cancer in June of 2011. We were all alone in our house, looking out of our bedroom at sailboats, white against blue, rushing into harbor. "It's late, isn't it?" she asked, coming in and out of morphine-assisted sleep. Those were her last words to me.

For years in my marriage, I counseled Susan about things to watch for after I got hit by the big bus in the sky. Things such as "Anything anyone wants to do for you, who can't explain themselves in a few simple paragraphs, should not be hired to help you," "Anything that seems like BS to you probably is," and, "You have to reach out to friends, not automatically assume that everyone is always going to call you." Of course, everything you plan for almost never happens the way you plan. It may be better than you anticipated. But it won't be as you thought or feared.

The first New Year's Eve I spent without her in 45 years was in 2011. That night, I was invited to dinner at an old friend's apartment in Boston, only about a mile from where I live, a walkable distance on the chilly, clear night. There is a grand fireworks display every New Year's Eve on Boston Common, where cows grazed during Revolutionary War times. It has been estimated that as many as 1 million people pour into the city to watch the show and stay for First Night festivities: mostly free performances for all the family, all over the city. I walked from my house, two blocks to Charles Street, a long thoroughfare bisecting the Common from the Public Garden, hundreds of thousands streaming toward the fireworks site. I said to myself, "How typical of my life, everyone moving toward the brilliant explosions. And me, moving in the opposite direction," even thinking, "I care much more about watching people's faces than seeing the sky lit up by fire." All of this, in my view, is part of the grief process. We were married for 45 years. But if anything is ever good in life, it's never long enough.

One of the themes in our marriage was always after various pronouncements on my part, Susan would respond with. . . "Grow up." Let's face it; women are the adults. Men are programmed to go out, kill the Brontosaurus, and bring home the steaks. And men habitually believe they're frozen in time at 18, despite all the signs to the contrary.

I never even looked back at the fireworks, happy to go against the grain. But I rejected all the clichés, such as "She's in a better place." I don't think so. Or "Life goes on." I say, "Define *life*." Of course, I was feeling sorry for myself, and not proud of it. The crowd pushed against me, families oohing and aahing with every explosion of sparkling lights, excited by the show, warmed in the freezing night, staying close to strangers.

Later that winter, I went to a birthday party for a high school classmate. One of the guests was a man, a doctor with the reputation of being the best internist in Boston: smart and caring. I knew that he had lost his wife some years before and had remarried. After dinner, he came up to me and said, "I'm so sorry about Susan. Of course we had heard. If you don't mind I'd like to tell you a little story."

"Sure," I answered.

"After my first wife died," the doctor said, "it was obviously very hard. And then I threw myself into work, buried myself in it. One day a patient came in to see me, an older Italian woman who still spoke with an accent after years in this country and always wore a black dress. She gave me her condolences, went through her examination, then left. About 10 minutes later she appeared in the office again.

"'Just a minute more of your time, please,' she said. 'Something I forgot.'

"She came in and asked me to sit down and I did. She stared at me for some time and then said, 'I thought you should hear this. She's not coming back.' Then she got up, pressed my hands briefly in hers. And left."

My initial reaction to what the Italian woman had said was that I wished the doctor had not told me that story. I didn't want to hear anyone say, "She's not coming back." Of course, the message he gave me was one of understanding life. But you have to be ready for messages, and often have to step back to appreciate the words in full.

I was almost 29 when we got married, and so much of what I know about life was drummed into me by my parents: history, standards, things to ponder and watch out for, and classics, such as "Debt can be a killer" and my mother's advice to my sister, "Never marry anyone prettier than you."

Most of you readers have never had to deal with a real personal loss, almost certainly not the loss of a spouse. But I will give you a life lesson that I have been preaching to people, clients, and friends, for many years. In a grieving situation, such as the death of a spouse, or more to your age situation, a divorce, it takes two years in your new incarnation to get used to the rhythm of that new life. No matter how prepared you are, how rich, how smart, how tough. It will take two years to understand what a life alone will mean to your daily routine and emotional stability. You cannot rush this process. And I have watched and counseled probably several thousand people in this situation. It will take two years to get a handle on your new reality. What you will spend? Whom can you trust? Can you reinvent yourself?

I have never been divorced and Susan has been gone for three years; I now know that I was right about the time frame. I still have hundreds of condolence notes on the dining room table. I still have most of her clothes, especially dresses and tailored jackets. Scarves and sweaters have been given to family and assorted special friends. Jewelry is still in a safe, pending sales or family distribution. Slacks and shoes are off to charity. You cannot rush the process; respect and ritual rule and there is a rhythm to grieving as there is to living one's life.

But after these two years, I now understand what the new normal is. And because I do not believe in retirement, it's as if I'm 29 years old again, only with some accumulated assets and many years of observing human nature: the good, the bad, and the occasionally very ugly.

I run an old-fashioned pain-in-the-neck business, and it operates seven days a week. It's a pain in the neck because it involves advice and counsel, not just about financial matters, but about many life decisions as well. They have included arranging to deliver a dead body from Spain to the United States for burial, getting a new credit card to Kathmandu for a student, calling the boyfriend of a client's daughter in South Africa to urge him not to break up with her, and getting bank credit for a great mystery writer who couldn't even get a loan from a loan shark. A pain-in-the-neck business, as I said. But incredibly rich in people and their stories. Some of these instructive stories, I hope, will make you look at your future in different ways, help you travel your new lives out of that nest of parents and teachers, and give you a guide for the many things that lie ahead of you. There will be practical solutions to building your team of the people you will need in key areas—legal, medical, and financial—and how to deal with bumps, such as losing a parent, divorce, raising children, getting fired, getting into clubs, sibling rivalry, getting plumbers and contractors to come on time, dealing with nonprofit boards, and a lot more. If I feel like I'm 29 again, I'm struck by how much I was clueless about at that time.

And what I've learned since then has been learned mostly by trial and error, the hard way.

I hope I can make your journeys a little easier with lessons about many new challenges where you're going to need fresh advice.

I want you to use this book as a plum pudding of ideas that may have never occurred to you. Reach in, pluck out a goodie, and tuck it away for your future.

PART I

BECOMING A PROFESSIONAL

CHAPTER 1

TAKE THE PRO TO LUNCH

I work in a big office, more than 200 people on two floors in the financial district of my city. The rookies sit in the boardroom, sometimes 15 to 20 of them, almost all late twenties to early thirties, all out in life, and all anxious. Occasionally, as I wander around the office to blow off steam, I'll stop, sit on a desk facing them, and talk to the young people informally, off-the-cuff, about how the money management business has changed over the years, what they should be paying attention to, and how to plan their future in the business. No one tells them these things. They hear nothing about institutional memory, what makes markets move beyond daily news bytes and how to really build a successful business and future.

Recently, one of the rookies came to see me in my office. "Can I come to work for you?" he asked.

"I'm flattered," I said. "But my team is complete for now. But I will come by occasionally and speak to you all."

"We don't get this stuff from anyone."

"What did you major in, in college?"

"Economics."

"That's too bad," I said. "I try to hire people who majored in the classics. Or in history, or English. I want to surround myself with young people who know something about the past. Because knowledge about the past will help you so much with your future."

I would suggest that all of you, no matter what jobs you have or jobs you want, seek out the oldest people in your present company, or the people who have worked there the longest. If they're still employed after long service, they must have something special to offer. So you should invite them to lunch, to *buy* them lunch. They'll be happy to do it and will tell you tales that will give you a different appreciation and insight into your business and the industry it's in. It will be much more valuable to you than most of the orientation and the too-often colorless meetings you attend regularly. These older people will be generous and important to your growth, because no one ever asks them to share their experiences, their histories. Often they might appear to be curmudgeons or seem intimidating. Set that aside and approach them graciously. They need the interchange as well, and will be very glad you asked them out.

It is important as you build a career to develop friends, both older and younger than you. The older ones can shape your development. The younger ones can keep you thinking young.

Take an old pro to lunch.

CHAPTER 2

BEWARE OF EXPERTS

By now you're getting the picture that street smarts trump all in the advice department. None of you probably, at your stage of life, is going to have intimate conversations with the chief executive officers of the Fortune 500 companies—unless you are related to them. So you will have to get your life wisdom from the seasoned professionals with whom you work, particularly the ones who can talk as mentors and teachers, not those who preach from on high. Most of my investment ideas come from my smart clients and friends around the world, not from Wall Street analysts or research departments.

One of my clients, Peter Clark, ran a think tank in Pittsburgh, mostly concentrating on the defense sectors. I spoke to him perhaps 20 years ago and asked whether he had seen a certain article in the *Wall Street Journal*.

"I haven't read a newspaper in 15 years," he told me, and this was the preference in news dissemination, because virtually every American read the papers.

"How can you not read newspapers?" I asked, surprised by his answer.

"Because 15 years ago I knew all about two subjects," he said. "And every time I read about those two subjects in the papers they always got it wrong, so I said to myself, 'If they're wrong about what I know, what about the stuff I don't know?' And I figured if I don't read the press, I'll save over an hour a day of wasted time!" Apply this to your own wanderings through the media, and don't accept anything just because it's in print or on your screen, in blogs or tweets.

For an even more personal brush with alleged brilliance, I was at a business dinner months before the meltdown of our financial system, sometime early in 2007. My parent company, Citibank, was coming to Boston in a big way, planning to open 30 new branches, and attacking the city for business in all the areas Citi wanted to dominate, including loans and wealth management.

Citi invited key local employees to a dinner and asked us to bring guests who might become major clients of the bank. We were to hear a dog and pony show from two Citi directors; one of them who had been secretary of the Treasury and was now a door opener for Citi business all over the world. His pay was in the millions of dollars for relatively small-time commitment. The two directors acted as if they were doing us all a huge favor by stooping to speak to us colonists in Boston. The words *superior attitude* did spring to mind. But the dinner and wine were free, and, on business evenings, I did, and do believe, that good accidents do happen sometimes. But you have to be there for the good accidents to happen.

I brought two guests, one man who ran a high-yield mutual fund, another who was a local commercial real estate developer, both lifelong Bostonians, not easily seduced by out of towners.

The two Citi directors did a Fric and Frac commentary about the wonders of the bank, speaking as if the Holy Grail were available for us if we came on board. This is fine, of course, their wanting us to drink the Kool-Aid. But the tone implied, "We know better than all of you about almost everything. Listen to us; watch us, the models for so much that is good and smart, and worthy."

One of my guests slipped me a folded piece of paper while the show rolled on. It said, "Neither of these two guys would know a real working American if they fell over one." Citibank stock during the financial crunch of 2007–2009 fell from approximately $55 a share to less than one dollar. Whenever you listen to someone who is billed as someone *you* could never be, take it with several grains of salt.

Beware the so-called experts and their absolute certainty about the future.

CHAPTER 3

IF YOUR COMPANY IS BOUGHT BY ANOTHER

I have been through dozens of mergers over 50 years, many of them shotgun marriages, with a lot of the companies we acquired done at bargain prices because the sellers were in desperate straits. One of these companies was quite famous in the investment world: E. F. Hutton. It had a campaign with the tagline for all the ads, "When E. F. Hutton talks, people listen." It was going broke. Right after the merger, my wife and I were going on a company trip. It was a relatively cheap junket, by Wall Street standards, to a resort in Florida in June, when all the tourist prices were slashed. On a chartered bus we sat with a bunch of former Hutton employees, all bitching and moaning about the stingy new owners. "Remember that great trip to Paris?" they would say. "No, Rome was much better, and also London: every night Michelin-starred restaurants."

My wife said to me, "Rome, London, Paris? We never went anywhere like that."

"They went broke," I said. "They're like a defeated army."

"Yeah," she said, "but they went broke in style."

Wall Street could always create products and sell them to the public for a fee. It could merchandise the goods. It could *not* run a business. Which is why so many great names on the Street turned to dust, and their names disappeared.

Almost always when you see the press stories surrounding every big merger, the two chief executive officers (CEOs) are pictured shaking hands, toasting, and celebrating the grand event. And they say, smiling, with reassuring tones, "*Nothing* will change." I will tell you that *everything will change*. It's the nature of mergers, like the losers and winners in wars. And there is no such thing as a marriage, or merger, of equals.

Machiavelli is still being read today, after 600 years. You should pay attention, of course, to your own careers and try to think in detached ways about this. If a merger of your company and another is announced, ask yourself, "Who is my rabbi, or protector, in this company, and is he or she likely to remain in a position of power?" If the answer to yourself is a bit shaky, I would drop the new CEO a personal note, and have it be a provocative one. It may, of course, be viewed as sucking up. And it is. But it is provocative, meaning in this sense, *different* from what most people would say, designed to make the recipient think, "Hmmm. . ." about you, getting you on his or her radar. How do you do that? Tell a little story about how you got hired, about an unusual hobby you have, a helpful observation about how something could be done better in the company, or something a client or customer suggested to you, showing your curiosity and enthusiasm about looking at problems in creative ways. The point is to separate yourself subtly from the crowd.

All mergers produce anxiety on both sides. Position yourself to be a personality, someone to be watched. Of course, you have to deliver, but first you have to plant a seed. And you plant it by being a little bit different.

There is no such thing as mergers of equals.

CHAPTER 4

ENTITLEMENT

If *entitlement* is not your least favorite word, it should be. This word is used a lot in modern American society, particularly among the new adults we all see. I know young people who before they've ever cashed a paycheck, have been helicopter skiing in Canada, windsurfing in the Bahamas, sailing in the Greek isles, staying in suites at the Bristol in Paris, and on safari in Tanzania.

This is not sour grapes. It's just my fear that these blessings early in life give these people the very false sense that all of their adult lives will be more of the same.

My father drummed into me, at an early age, one of his favorite lines, "Just remember, life is really hard, punctuated by moments of brilliance." And I now think this was right. He carried it to extremes, however. If he was given a new sweater for a present, he would not put it on until he had a day where he deemed himself worthy. Deprivation, because of superstition, is not a very healthy quality.

I went to college with a group of guys I called "the golden boys." They were handsome, successful on the athletic fields and in their social lives, and comfy in their natural sense of superiority, in their belief that their lives after college would be a continuation of their early privileged childhoods. Life would be one continuous coming–out party. For almost all the golden boys, this was their finest hour, and life after school proved to be one disappointment after another. They found it very difficult to shake off childhood and reinvent themselves.

I contrast this with the story of a young man who came to see me recently, having found me on some Internet search. He was a sophomore at a local college and wanted to apply for an internship in our office. I'm a sucker for listening to and talking with young people. They help me with managing money because they clue me in to their buying and spending habits, and what they think of the future. And what scares them. When I am around young men and women with fire in the belly, it gives me hope for the future.

This young man grew up in Miami. "My dad had a manufacturing business, specialty plastics. I always thought, 'No heavy lifting for me. Life is sweet. Just follow him, join the biz and *la vida loca*. Then came 2008 and the financial meltdown and Dad's business evaporated. It's as if our lives and happy family melted away."

But he took it as a wake-up call, taking jobs after school, starting a T-shirt business, enrolling in Chinese language courses, and raising money for neighborhood causes. Early in college life he threw himself into the other part-time jobs, and pestering businesspeople in our city for "15 minutes of wisdom."

He told me, "Having the hell scared out of me at an early age, and having all my assumptions about life turned upside down, made me realize that it was on *me*. I have to do it myself. Visiting the Sistine ceiling in Rome can wait until I pay for it, and I will."

A sense of entitlement will sooner or later take you down.

CHAPTER 5

DON'T BE A WISE GUY

I have seen many hotshots come and go in my working life, people arriving at my firm with big reputations, the cocks of the walk. Almost always they never live up to the hype. I remember a number of these people. One of them demanded that a special office be carved out for himself, with part of the floor where his outsized desk sat raised above the level of the rest of his office. It was like a throne room, so he could look down on and intimidate visitors. He drove a Bentley and chased the sales assistants. He was a great salesman, in the days when the entire stock brokerage business was commission based. If you did not have your customers trading in and out on a regular basis, you had no revenue. If a customer of his objected to his advice to sell something a couple of weeks after buying it, he would say, "I'm the captain. When the captain says, 'Sell,' you sell."

At quiet moments he would tell me, "I was *meant* to be in this business. I feel that I really *know,* know what I'm saying? I really *know.*"

In my experience, anytime in my career when I'm tempted to say to myself, "You really *know,*" it means that I'm about to have my tail handed to me, and that there are things out there I haven't figured out. Bad behavior and arrogance always get paid back, and not in good ways. The hotshot in my office hopped firms a lot, and ultimately was sued by a variety of clients and forced to leave the business, banned for life, the throne room carved into three separate offices. I recall the mentality at the old Lehman Brothers retail offices, with whom we were merged. A manager there actually said to his troops, "Boys, just remember, a customer is like a garbage bag. . . Fill 'em up. And toss 'em out." Many of their salespeople were contemptuous of others who put the clients first and believed in long-term relationships. I was not surprised in the least when Lehman Brothers crashed and burned and disappeared. The greed in management seeps in poisonous ways through the whole system.

Toast your successes by all means. Look at your trophies, your medals, and your plaques, and remember those moments and what got you there. I have a little mantra that has kept me from getting too excited when triumphs appear. I look at a small medal I've kept since the eighth grade. It has a baseball player etched onto one side and on the other, *American Legion Champs, 1951*. Our seventh-grade town team had lost all eight games the previous year. In the *eighth* grade we went eight and zero, with all the same players from the year before. I look at the medal and say, "Dreams of glory." And I say it with a smile, knowing that glory gets snatched from us many times in life. Savor the moment but never say to yourself, "Now I *really* know what it's all about." Because you never *will* know what it is all about, and an ironic attitude about the good *and* the bad will serve you well.

Nobody likes a wise guy, and the knives will be out for you if you are.

CHAPTER 6

A LITTLE BIT OF NEW JERSEY OR BROOKLYN

I was talking to one of my partners about a friend in our business, who intellectually, could run rings around most people. This friend was very well educated in the Ivy League and in England. He understood the financial markets and loved researching ideas. But he had a modest business and not much luck in bringing in new clients. "He needs a bit of New Jersey in him," my partner said, who grew up in New Jersey, street-smart.

It is tough to teach someone to be more aggressive, to punch the greed button in someone else. But we are *all* in sales in one way or another, whether in politics, religion, development, or any profession. A young lawyer friend of mine called me recently and said, "You were right."

"About what?" I asked.

"You tried to get me to be a financial advisor years ago, and I told you, 'I hate to sell anything, I just can't do it.' Now I want to be a partner in my law firm and management tells me, 'If you want to make partner you're going to have to bring a lot more new business than you're doing now.'

"I didn't realize it years ago," he said, "but I guess we're all in sales in one way or another."

The best salespeople I've ever met in financial markets could make everyone they talked with greedy; they could verbally paint dreams, dreams that they could convince others would come true. The best stockbroker salesman I ever knew would tell prospective clients, "Do yourself a favor; buy some of this for your mother." This pitch did two things. It made the buyer think it was conservative enough for an elderly person and think if that were true, it should also be a sure thing.

If you've been in business for some time, you've built up scar tissue. This comes from being disappointed, from being fired, from disillusions with management, or from any number of things that make you wonder, "What's out there for me?"

One of my best friends went to Hollywood after college to seek his fortune. All our friends and I knew he'd be a huge hit in Hollywood. He was successful, living by his wits and energy and a belief in himself that wouldn't quit. But the Oscars, Golden Globes, and hit series eluded him. One night almost 25 years ago, we had dinner in Hollywood. After a few drinks he said to me, "You know why my name isn't in the lights on the hillside? I came out here educated at private schools in Philadelphia, boarding school in New England, Ivy League college. And while I was writing thank-you notes to various hostesses for weekends in Palm Springs, the kids from Brooklyn who didn't go to college and hitchhiked out here, were going by me like a shot. My edges were too rounded off." I told this story to a client of mine, David Susskind, who had one of the most successful talk/interview shows on television in the 1970s and 1980s.

"Well," he said, "I was never shy. Full of anxiety, sure. But I learned early in this business to show no weakness to the outside world. They'll murder you if you show weakness. And one other thing that I think everyone has to learn if they're out in the world: if you believe in yourself, it's okay once in a while to be a little pushy."

It's okay to be a little pushy, and you have to learn this the hard way.

CHAPTER 7

DON'T BE AFRAID TO ASK STUPID OR PROVOCATIVE QUESTIONS

We're all insecure in certain ways. Even the richest and most powerful people on the planet have secret fears and self-doubts they would never share with the public or the media. I have had chief executive officers of large companies say to me in moments of confession, "I often felt during my career that I was a complete fraud, in totally over my head. But I wouldn't tell anyone; 'Show no weakness' has to be the mantra. Or you're finished."

All of us go to meetings in our businesses and professions. Every business has a jargon all its own, with acronyms rampant. People who have been in the company longer than you know all the acronyms. You hear the acronyms in meetings and have no idea what they stand for, but you don't want to appear clueless. So you nod as if you completely get it, spend the rest of the meeting wondering if you'll ever be in with the in crowd, and you lose your sense of the meeting's flow.

My mind wanders in meetings, especially when people drone on just to go on the record as saying *something,* anything to prove they're awake, even if it adds nothing substantive. If you're running a meeting, assume that not everyone knows those acronyms. Don't gloss over them if you're the boss.

Raise your hand if you're new to the company. "What does SA mean?" I once asked.

"Sorry, *sales assistant,* I thought you would know," someone said to me when the term was bandied about and I had no idea: it was a new company for me, and where I came from everyone still used *secretary.*

Titles are meaningless in my view, but perception is everything in corporate life, which is increasingly governed by human resources departments and compliance as over regulation and bureaucracy run rampant. In the early 1990s my company took a corporate tent at a U.S. Open golf tournament. One of the days of the event, I went there with a friend from the office. We were both senior vice presidents of the firm. After spending the morning watching the tournament, we went to the firm's tent to have some lunch. Going up to the table in front, run by half a dozen young women hired for the occasion, we said, "Lunch for two, please."

After asking for our credentials the young woman checked the list. "Your names are not here. This is lunch for only institutional clients and the bankers."

"We're senior vice presidents of the firm," my friend said indignantly.

"Hey," the woman said, "we've got *hundreds* of those."

We were turned away. As George Orwell said, "Some pigs are more equal than others."

As we walked away my friend said, "Typical corporate idiots."

"Wait here," I said to him, and walked back to the table.

"Yes?" the young woman asked.

"Does it make sense to you that I'm an officer of the firm, and their name is on this tent, and they spent hundreds of thousands of dollars to entertain here, and that lunch cost them for two *maybe* $25, and that the firm probably doesn't want to alienate two key employees for $25?"

"On the list, or not on the list. That's my orders."

"I know you're doing your job. But I've come a long way for this event and the boss here is going to be very happy to see me. If you could give him this note, please." She did deliver it. And it said, "I'm incredibly close to Putnam and Fidelity and I can help cement these relationships." I enclosed my card. Those two mutual funds were among the firm's biggest clients in Boston. A man, based in New York, whom I did not know came out from the tent.

"Frank and Billy are good friends of mine," I said. "The head traders at those two funds. Two chicken salad sandwiches is what it will cost you. Maybe two beers, for a lot of goodwill."

He looked at my card suspiciously but motioned to me and my pal to come in. "What the hell," he said, "it's a better story than I could've told," ushering us in with the in crowd.

The young woman at the desk and I told each other, "Have a good day."

And we did.

**No can turn to yes if you approach others
in original ways.**

CHAPTER 8

LAUGHTER CAN DIFFUSE THE PROBLEMS

Americans, more than most peoples of the world, love to talk about themselves. We feel a great need to unload on others. I've always thought that you should give it up to very, *very* few people and that you should always be somewhat of a mystery to others.

For instance, we all greet each other every day with, "How are you?" "How you doin'?" and "What's up?"

"Fine," "Great," "Doin' well," "Fantastic." Knee-jerk questions and knee-jerk answers. Most people don't really care how you are, and anyone answering, "Fantastic" is probably *far* from that condition.

When people ask me, "How are ya?" I answer, "Every day is an adventure, and some of the adventures are really good."

The answer is always true. Every day *is* an adventure and no one else will have this answer. It's neutral, saying nothing, really. But different as well. And you want to be different.

You cannot force *funny,* but you can learn to diffuse difficult business situations by bringing smiles into the equation. It *can* solve problems. For instance: last fall there was a longtime client in his mid-eighties who ran a large margin account (borrowing against his assets to buy more stock). Our legal compliance department wanted to talk with him about appropriate behavior, meaning, "You're in your eighties. Do you really know what you're doing? Leveraging yourself with so much debt? At your age?"

All you people out there thinking of going into the investment business in any capacity should know that the lawyers took over Wall Street around 2002. This escalated in the financial meltdown starting in 2007 and has resulted in oversight overkill since then. Big Brother *and* Sister are definitely watching. My chief assistant called the client to give him a heads-up that Compliance was going to give him a call to make sure he understood the risks involved in borrowing against stocks.

He hit the roof. "I'm in my eighties—I've been running other people's money for more than 60 years. And I continue to run my own money, successfully I might add. I know more about risk than any rookie reading out of a rules handbook will ever know. How dare anyone call me to check to see if I'm out of my mind, as if I lost my marbles. I'm going to transfer my money elsewhere."

"I'll let them know," my assistant said. "You know that there are all kinds of rules and regulations since the financial meltdown. We can't help it."

"Doesn't mean I have to put up with this foolishness. I'm going somewhere with common sense. No one is going to legislate human nature with me."

My assistant told me about this problem. I hate to lose business over regulation overkill, scalp hunting.

"I'll call him," I said.

"Albert (not his real name)," I said to the client, "you owe yourself a treat."

"How's that?" he asked, suspicious.

"You're going to get a call from the Compliance Department. And you're furious. Look at it a little differently. The woman who is going to call you is a rookie. Don't shoot the messenger. You can have some fun with this. Educate her about human nature versus bureaucracy. Teach her something about age and experience, and how over 60 is not dead."

"Okay, good point," he said. "Maybe I can help her in her job."

Later he called me back. "I think I'm in love," he said. "And I also think we both learned something. Me, that we're in regulation hell.

She, that we're free to do what we want with our own money, even if sometimes it's foolish."

A little humor and humanity can solve problems and bring people back to the table.

CHAPTER 9

YOU NEVER KNOW ANYONE UNTIL YOU DEAL WITH THEIR MONEY

Years ago someone made me a needlepoint pillow with the words that frame this chapter. You never *do* really know anyone until you deal with their money, because money brings out the best in people and the worst in people. And you can never really tell which it will be until they're in the room, the deal, or the bed with you. People have come to see me who had the reputation of being brutal, impossible. And once they were in the program, they were pussycats, seldom ever even calling unless nudged. The reverse is true in spades. People who seemed, in the interview process, to be lovely, gentle people, became impossible to deal with, cranky, nasty, and dismissive to my support staff. Nothing like they appeared to be. So don't assume anything if you're in the professions that deal with others' money or souls: law, medicine, real estate, clergy, and sales of all kinds. Not just money management. It's like advice my father gave me, good advice: "Never count anyone else's money. You'll be wrong in *both* directions."

So don't assume anything in areas where emotion comes to the forefront. You will get lots of good surprises. And bad surprises.

Early in my writing career (I've had two full-time jobs for all my working life), I had a number of brushes with Hollywood. People wanting to buy or option books of mine. I got a lot of promises that sent me reeling from meetings with visions of Krugerrands spilling from my pockets and beach houses in Malibu. For instance, Mel Brooks at a lunch with him, told me, "Don't worry, kid, I'll take care of you." And I never heard from him again. But I learned: never spend it until it is in your pockets.

It pays to be optimistic, but keep a grain of suspicion in there, too.

CHAPTER 10

PLAN FOR THE *WORST* CASE, NOT THE *BEST,* IN BUSINESS AND IN LIFE

It's difficult to try to make decisions with your brain and not your heart or stomach. Planning anything seems to go with the same thing: optimistic projections, somewhat pie-in-the-sky, best case on into the future. I see dozens of business plans a year from people eager to start new ventures and asking my advice about them. And I'm not in the deal business. Partly because all new ventures involve meetings. I cannot stand meetings. So much time is wasted on participants making sure they chime in with their own meanderings just to go on record as saying *something,* to show they're awake. Is this too cynical for you? I've been going to meetings for more than 50 years, and the only ones I found valuable were the ones that taught me something I never knew before. Such as the time the chairman of our board described in detail what it was like to do business with Saudi Arabia. I came away from that meeting thinking that nothing has changed in thousands of years in the Middle East and that stripping all the nonsense away, it's all about power . . . and money, and thinking that the sand is softer in the country next door.

As an aside to this planning chapter, avoid corporate clichés, such as *going forward* or *break down the silos,* wherever possible. These expressions are only signs of lack of original corporate thinking. The latest corporate-speak I've heard, on a trip to Manhattan, was, "I don't have enough bandwidth for this." Since then I've heard *bandwidth* a number of times. Make up your own comments, and, when they prove popular in business, abandon them for new ones. Other old ones are *best-case* and *worst-case.* I find most business plans worthless. And I've seen plans that seemed flawless. But the creators of these plans often cannot raise the money to put them into effect. These plans are all useless unless you find the money. I learned this lesson early in business. When I was first registered to sell and buy securities for clients, I would make lists on yellow legal pads of friends, former classmates, relatives, and everyone I could think of who would surely give me business. *None* of them gave me business. Not one. All had the same excuses: "You're not experienced enough," "I've already got someone," and "I never do business with friends. Why risk a friendship if your picks don't work for me?" I found the best clients came from brand-new relationships, strangers. They had no history with me and no preconceptions from the past. Strangers have become my biggest supporters and best bird dogs for new clients. Learn early about human nature: many friends, family members, too, sometimes have a stake in *not* wanting you to succeed, even though they would never admit it.

Someone very close to me, years ago, sold his wife on a new career for himself in specialty sales. Some would have said, a pyramid scheme. He left a career that had been professionally successful, then hit some bumps. But he was seduced emotionally by a charismatic entrepreneur who infused him with energy and the impossible dreams.

"Look," he was told, "pour your focus into this. Treat it like law school. Three years to set yourself and your family free." My friend told his wife, "Three years and we'll have a house in town and a house on the shore in South Carolina. We can do everything you ever wanted, me around, travel, money flowing in for our lifetime as I build my network. Others working for us."

He tried to recruit me and my children in his sales efforts. "Nothing in life will set you free in three years," I told him. "It's a pipe dream that will end in tears."

It did. His marriage broke up. He owns no house and still struggles in life. Sad.

Don't project easy money. Don't spend it until it's in your pocket. Best-case predictions seldom come true. And for almost whatever you plan, in business or the cost of building a new garage, it will cost you more money and take more time than you thought.

Sure, do a business plan that promises riches for you and the investors into the sunset. But, don't be taken in by your own wishful-thinking projections. Secretly, figure from the business plan, *worst* case. If you can survive that, good for you. Best case is for dreamers.

Hope for the best, but make sure you understand the *worst* case as well.

CHAPTER 11

SO YOU WANT TO BE IN THE INVESTMENT BUSINESS

This is a business in which there are many ways to the truth, endless interesting possibilities, and a profession that is not in decline; it grows with the population, now more than 320 million people in America. And no matter what technology brings us, people need, and will *always* need, advice and counsel about their money. The majority of us cannot do this on our own. The more personal and old-fashioned you can make this advice, the busier and more successful you will be.

I'll concentrate here on what it takes to advise and counsel clients on the wealth management side. But there are endless areas to participate in the business of money. There is old-fashioned banking, lending. Within banking there is trading, the buying and selling of securities and sophisticated derivatives. There are trust departments, offering personal services to clients and training programs to get you initiated. There are back office and support areas, research departments, human resources, legal and compliance, information technology, all growing as rules and regulations layer complexity into every workday. The job possibilities are endless and generally well paying.

I like businesses where the upside for you as individuals is unlimited. Direct money management is one of those professions, perfect for the lone wolves and people who essentially work for themselves and their clients, no matter what company name is on the door. This is a job for entrepreneurs.

If you come into this wealth management, understand that it will take you three to five years to know whether you'll be any good at this business. It's ironic that many training programs will cut you off much sooner than that, as soon as you don't meet certain benchmarks that, in my opinion, are almost impossible to reach unless you're a born aggressive salesperson or have a rich family that feeds you business. Virtually every really successful wealth manager I have known took a long time to develop a big practice and years before each found his or her real niche. Eventually, often longer than a three- to five-year time frame, each discovered that groove. And whenever I would annually meet with my peers around the country, *every* one of the big-time producers had a different specialty. Some focused on bonds, some on picking outside managers; some picked their own stocks, and some did alternative investments: real estate, hedge funds, and mergers and acquisitions.

It would help also if you could find a mentor in this learning process, someone producing business and *not* in management. Mentors in America seem to be a dying art in the age of the self-absorbed or where the attention span is a snap of the fingers. I trained in a boardroom populated with stockbrokers of all ages and abilities. Clients sat on chairs in the boardroom as well, characters. They sat and kept each other warm, and amused. There was *life* in the boardroom. Clients watched the ticker tape and traded stocks and stories. And they all taught the rookies, with advice and opinions, not just about stocks and bonds. But also about life.

The most important quality you would need, more than anything else in the wealth management business, is being good with people. If you can sell yourself and you play well with others, you can always make a living.

Also be insatiable about asking questions of people seasoned in the business. Be relentless in seeking a mentor. Do not blindly accept training manuals or training protocol, and don't be afraid to be unconventional in your thinking as long as you are willing to work harder than your fellow trainees. Smart management will notice your going the extra mile.

And get copies of Adam Smith's *The Money Game,* Brutus's *Confessions of a Stockbroker,* and *Liar's Poker* by Michael Lewis. These are classic books on the money business. Classic in revealing to you that human nature never changes, regardless of ever-changing technology and fads.

If you are good with people, it's the most important element for success in the investment business.

CHAPTER 12

DO YOUR HOMEWORK

A young woman came to see me recently, a development (money-raising) person, delegated to making the case for me to make a gift to the nonprofit she represented. I was on the board of the organization and had been for some time. She went right into her pitch, extolling the virtues of the nonprofit's mission and the people it served.

"Do you have a clue into *anything* about me?" I asked. "Assume nothing when you're asking strangers for money. Who am I and what do I care about in life?"

"Well," she said, surprised by my opening salvo. "You've been on the board and generous over the years."

I find that being a surprise to people almost always sucks them into knowing that this is not the usual interview and that perhaps we can both learn something. It's good also to temper what could be seen as a hostile opening with something softer and encouraging.

"Tell me a little bit about yourself," I said. We all love to talk about ourselves. It's partly why therapies of all kinds are a national sport in America.

The young woman smiled and was off to the races, happy to be chatting about her background, schools, and hobbies.

When she was done, I told her what I was going to pledge to her organization. "But in the future," I told her, after spinning a few stories about my own life and interests, "do your homework about the people you're scheduled to meet, *before* you see them." Google is a good start, or a coworker who may know the character you're seeing. Particularly get some trivia or odd fact. If you bring it up, it flatters the person you're seeing and because of this you'll be more likely to succeed in the new relationship, and you may even get more money out of them, if *that's* what you're seeking.

In meetings with new people make sure you have a clue about who they are and what may be their passions.

CHAPTER 13

HOW TO GET GOOD PRESS AND PUBLICITY

I've been doing book tours and interviews for more than 45 years, and I almost always came away with great results. Even better, many of the people who have interviewed me became friends, setting the stage for easy, not snarky, interviews and callbacks in the future.

I have a friend who has been on the *Forbes* 400 richest people in America list for years. He has also been very much in the public eye.

"How the hell do you always get good press?" he once asked me. "I get slammed much more than I get praised." He thought a bit then added, "As a matter of fact, I seldom get a good interview."

I knew him well enough to say, "That's because it's all about you, all the time."

"That's a bunch of bull," he answered. Then a small smile.

"If you want to get good press and have people want to like you," I told him, "try asking the interviewer, on pauses in the process, about their own lives: where they grew up, do they have children. What was their first job after college? People want that human touch. They want to be valued. In your case, even if you *don't* give a damn about the person scribbling in a notebook or punching on a recording device, force yourself to think about the person asking the questions. You're going to get better press. And it very well might make you a better person, not just a richer one."

We all want to be valued as human beings. Don't treat interviewers as if they're robots, only interested in *you*.

Always interview the interviewer if you want good press.

CHAPTER 14

ACTS OF KINDNESS

There are seemingly simple things out there that can improve your business lives. These fall in the category of "you never know."

I went to a cocktail party some years ago. There were about 100 people there. It was summer: a lot of silk dresses, men in khaki suits, blazers, a few guys in seersucker, lawyers and bankers, money people, and real estate types. One of the guests had just sold his private company to a Fortune 500 giant, setting this guest free, financially, not to continue working if he chose. The news was prominent in the financial press. The guest was not a good friend but a really good acquaintance at the time, and I was honestly so pleased with his news. He was very smart and what I would call "cool": well turned out, thoughtful, it seemed to me, about life around him. I congratulated him on the news, and he went on about the long process and layers of opinion that went into the sale. He was very interested in the human nature side of the story, the dance of negotiations and the egos involved. Then we drifted away into other conversations, although he asked me what I thought of the current stock market. I mentioned the concept of something I called the "Vulture Fund."

My father had taught me this idea. When stock markets were depressed and energy shares were particularly out of favor, my dad would buy a package of single-digit oil and gas issues on what was then the American Stock Exchange; two-, three-, and four-dollar stocks are totally speculative, not blue chips. "Sooner or later the worm turns," my father told me. "Happiness is a thousand shares of a three-dollar stock in America. Half your list will double when that worm turns. Then you sell 'em and wait for another chance."

The man who had sold his company bought into this concept of the Vulture Fund. He became a client eventually, and a treasured friend. He does not suffer fools well, is demanding of himself, and wants anyone deserving of his trust to be creative in his or her thinking. Acts of kindness involve being generous of spirit in an honest way. They can also lead to relationships that can be important to you in many ways. Be pleased about people's success. You never know.

Be honestly good to people. You will never know how your kindness can enhance your life.

CHAPTER 15

TIPPING

I've always been a generous tipper. I know, originally, it was because after my junior year in college, I worked on Cape Cod as a busboy in a popular restaurant. The busboys received 15 percent of the waitresses' tips each night, which we pooled between us. I never forgot how much the waitresses would complain about people who shortchanged them or stiffed them altogether. They all worked hard and came from modest means. I've learned over the years that in business and life, you get more out of people with honey than with vinegar. Tipping the right way can make certain adventures in life a lot easier for you. It's a cost of business and a pleasure, too, that you should do with grace and humor.

My friend George was in the women's shoe-manufacturing business, an industry long gone from America. They called themselves the "shoe-ies" and they were a rambunctious, high-energy lot. They were big gamblers, too, high rollers. Because every season they had to gamble on the styles that might be popular: the skins, the heel heights, the colors, the sizes, and the markets. Most of them also were highly leveraged, meaning borrowing of money to finance their always-risky operations. They liked the good life as well and always needed to be taken care of wherever they traveled on business. They traveled a lot: to shoe shows, to factories in Italy, and eventually to the Far East, where labor costs were much lower than in the United States. George was smooth, with slicked-back hair, and charming, with an original patter that disarmed people and won them to his side. When people would ask him, as they ask all of us, "How are you?" George would say, "A lot *you* care." No one ever said that, and it drew people in.

He taught me how to "Duke" people so that you always got the best tables in restaurants, upgrades to first class on flights, and tickets to hot shows or concerts. Years ago when George operated, tipping people with cash was rare outside of New York and, perhaps, show biz places, such as Los Angeles.

"In New York," George told me, "the first time in a restaurant I gave the maître d' a 10-spot." (That's like $50 today, figuring inflation.) "When I came in, I'd tell him, 'This is because I like your style.' After the first time, I'd make him wait for it until we left, give him a little anticipation, he'd put on the service to make sure he earned it. I do the same thing in hotels with the concierge. Give him a $10 bill, crisp and new. When I arrived, let him know 'just in case' I needed his services.

"After the first visit I'd Duke him when we left. Always make them wonder if they're going to earn it. They'd compete to get me good show tickets, good restaurant rez." George would do this with check-in clerks at airline counters, the boss at parking garages, and a certain salesman at Filene's Basement when they had primo merchandise on deep discount. The salesman would hide certain things for George, such as Armani cashmere jackets for $80 and Bill Blass blazers for $40. George Duked everyone, and he did it with charm and man-to-man, as if it were special, not as if he were some big bucks, sleazy guy whose money would buy him very little, or no, respect. It was the money, yes. But he also acted as if he respected and liked the recipient. Tip with innocence, as if it's a miracle that you've made any money yourself.

Tip people with a smile and a story, so they'll remember you, not just the money.

CHAPTER 16

RESUMES REDUX

I've written about resume preparation in the past. But always for people new to the process after college and grad school. This subject needs tweaking for you new adults as well.

Most of you have changed jobs in your careers, some of you several times. How do you stay fresh on paper and present yourselves in new ways that never seem desperate to interviewers? They can sense body language and certain anxieties. When they do sense these things, you're not going to get the job.

I have a college classmate who is a professor at Harvard Business School. He's a dramatically engaging speaker, able to transmit his passions to any audience lucky enough to hear him speak. His specialty is technology. In my last book, I talked about wanting to see on every resume something out of the ordinary, something that jumps off the page at the interviewer or the reader. One of the areas includes sports or interests that are not necessarily in the mainstream, such as rowing, rugby, women's ice hockey, or water polo. "My son was going for a new job interview," my professor classmate said to me. "I read your book and called my son. 'Read this book,' I told him. 'You *rowed*. Put it on your resume.'" He did and the young man got the job.

You have to look at the world these days in different, more creative, ways to make an impact in a society with a limited attention span. You have to make an impression.

One young woman was referred to me from a client recently. She was looking for a job in financial services. She had a good academic record and had done an internship with a regional bank, no heavy lifting. Her resume was without that spark that separated her from so many other applicants. I told her about the odd specialties that would help. And I mean being honest about these things, not making them up or fudging.

"I'm looking for something that jumps out at me on your resume. Plain vanilla isn't going to do it these days," I told her. As I asked her about hobbies and interests, she told me that she played lacrosse.

"What position?" I asked.

"Attack," she said.

"Ah," I answered. "Here's a secret about presenting yourself to others no matter what the medium. Add a bit of legitimate spice to your life in print. 'Played *attack* in lacrosse.' It means much more to the reader, it defines you better. I want to hire someone in sales for me who played *attack*."

If I graduated with honors in college and wrote a thesis, I'd say, "Honors. Senior thesis on the mysteries of Joseph Conrad." Give color to your life. Many of us are *not* boring. Get your foot in the door, and then show them what you've got. But you have to get your foot in the door.

If you want to get a job, add some legitimate spice to your resume.

CHAPTER 17

ALWAYS HAVE A FALLBACK PLAN

I recently had dinner with my two accountants, partners in a very personal, practical association. One of them told me about jobs he'd had in high school and college. He bussed tables and made ice cream sodas and sundaes. He did odd jobs for neighbors. When he was old enough he was a waiter and bartender. "Both my partner and I," he told me, "love to drink one of my creations, which I call a 'California Daydream.' It's apricot brandy, orange juice, topped with amaretto, shaken with ice and a cherry on top. Delicious." Both he and his partner ordered it made for themselves.

The waiter returned and said, "Sorry, gentlemen. We have no apricot brandy."

Without skipping a beat my friend said, "Got peach schnapps? It'll do if you have that."

Amazingly to me, the restaurant had peach schnapps.

My friend smiled. "In life," he said, "always have a fallback plan going in."

For any venture you're attempting, it's a very good suggestion, whether for a cocktail or a high-powered merger. It can apply to almost everything.

**Never assume every plan you hatch will work out;
prepare for what's next.**

CHAPTER 18

BLOOD AND WATER

If you work for a company where family is at the top, and you are *not* family, never think that you will ultimately move into the chief executive officer (CEO) slot. One of the largest mutual fund companies in the world is family controlled. I know three people who were presidents of the company over the years. All of them, it had been reported to me, felt confident that eventually the torch would be passed to them, and they would be the chosen CEO. Not one of them ever made it, and they all moved on to significant jobs in other places. Family businesses, large and small, can be nightmares. But they can be good, strong lessons for outsiders. If you work for a family in a small business and the owner is a benevolent dictator, it can be a great experience, with good pay and benefits and employees cared for and caring as well. Usually though, when the benevolent dictator dies, the inheriting family members can turn it all to dust, and everything can change for the worse.

If the family company is a large one, the dictator will have a court, just like ancient kings and emperors had a court. The courtiers typically are played off each other for the sport of the king, keeping them on edge and competitive. The courtiers tend to dislike each other strongly, jockeying for favor and elevation of their status. I would say working in a family business when you are *not* family would be a great opportunity to take notes or keep a journal on the experiences there. It will serve you well if only to remind you of the often-unbelievable things you will witness, and the things you can avoid in your next job.

The classic tale I've witnessed on this score was in the high-stakes American corporate world. One of the largest companies of its kind,

New York Stock Exchange, dominant in its field in many ways, had as its CEO a powerful man. The CEO, before he assumed that role, was in the corporate wilderness for a while, having lost a power struggle at a previous company. While searching for his next adventure, he hired as his chief assistant a young man just out of business school who was the son of a friend of the executive. The executive bought control of another public company, and he and the loyal young man worked incredibly close together, forging a bond almost like a father and son relationship. They worked together for more than 20 years, building the base for a very strong, highly successful, and even loving partnership. At some point after reaching critical mass and the acclaims of Wall Street and markets, the CEO's daughter was hired, with a senior job to do. But it proved to be a bumpy ride, and the disciple was senior to the daughter. In time he became critical of her performance and she eventually left. As I've said, he was the star and the heir apparent at the global company. But he, too, after some time was let go. Why, how could such an anointed one be cast off? Human nature. I'm imagining a conversation between the CEO and his dear wife after their daughter quit the company.

"The guy's days are numbered," said the wife to the husband.

"Not going to happen," said the CEO, "too valuable."

But every evening when the CEO came home, he would hear, "Is he *still* there?" She would refuse to use his name.

Eventually the CEO got worn down and the surrogate son thrown out of the boat to sink or swim on his own. Instant manhood. No protector.

It was a classic business and life error. *Never* disrespect the boss's daughter, or the sons, if they are in the company. Sooner or later blood will trump all, and Dad will *always* choose his little girl over *you* no matter how good you are.

If you join the family business and you're not family, don't delude yourself that someday you'll be in charge.

CHAPTER 19

MEDIA TRANSLATIONS

You have already read a lot in the media about the crisis in American education. We don't have enough students concentrating in mathematics and sciences. Often what we read about what I call the "Oh, my Gods," which prove to have nothing to do with what we should *really* worry about. The Oh, my Gods are headlines about the horrors happening daily in the world or the many predicted disasters over the years, for example, the headlines about the Y2K moment when all computer systems would crash and the headlines in the early 1980s about the Japanese taking over the world. Just in time to go into a 20-year depression. What really damages us are the bolts from the blue that no one could foresee: Pearl Harbor, 9/11, and the Kennedy assassination. It's a total surprise in life that can damage us the most, not the inflammatory headlines. As for the daily news here's the first lesson: in a conversation years ago I had with a good friend, a consultant, I asked him whether he'd seen a certain article recently in the *Wall Street Journal*.

"I haven't read a newspaper in years," he said. This is the man who, as mentioned in Chapter 2, found that whenever he read about two subjects that he knew all about in the press, it always got them wrong, which caused him to stop reading newspapers. He planted the seed. And every time I read stories about subjects I think I understand, I agree that the press seldom gets them right. Just be skeptical about what you read, and try not to accept at face value what you gather from the many sources of information. As an aside, *every* political ad describing the candidate's opponent is *always* misleading. In election years, if you tune those out, you can save yourself a lot of time.

The second lesson concerns misconception in practical solutions. Once again it involves press coverage. There has been much dire prediction for some time that not enough American students are focusing on math and sciences and that we are falling way behind other countries in these crucial areas. Smart friends of mine, a New York couple, recently visited Tunisia. They were on a mission to a training center that educated poor Arab children in the important things to get them jobs in the future. The man running the program was a senior person at Microsoft. One of my friends surprised me when he said, "Microsoft runs much of their administrative network in Europe through Tunisia."

"So Microsoft thinks they can predict the jobs of the future? And focuses, of course on science and math," I said.

"You're going to be shocked," he said. "The man told me two-thirds of the jobs in the future haven't been invented yet. No one knows what they're going to be. Forget science and math. What's going to get these kids the jobs of the future is one thing: *communication,* verbally and in writing. You will have to interact with others socially. Those two communication skills will get these kids jobs, no matter *what* gets invented. The skills are what we teach the children. Collaboration with others is key."

Almost never accept conventional wisdom.

CHAPTER 20

SO YOU GOT FIRED

Relationships of all kinds are challenged whenever the economics of society decline, when hard times hit. Millions of worthy, hardworking people lose their jobs. We're in that mode today. The good news for you younger readers: from 25 to 45, if you lose a job, you're eminently employable if you follow some practical hints. The bad news for so many 55 and older is that you feel young. But the cruel world of employment can make you feel as if you're damaged goods. This is a horrible downside in American culture geared so much to the young. My last book, *No One Ever Told Us That,* has been published in foreign editions in China, Japan, and Korea. But not in Europe. Why? Because it's street-smart advice to graduates of college from a grandfather. Eternal thoughts, not geared to fads or passing popular obsessions. The Far East, with thousands of years of history, values experience and wisdom passed down from endless generations much more than the Western world does. We are a society obsessed with youth, social networking, and slimmer figures. It's what the mirror tells us much more than what we need to learn to grow and prosper.

My friend Andy Hunter is one of the best in the business known in common parlance as headhunting. I wanted his take on the subject he deals with daily.

"Let's be clear about a few things," he said. "You spend maybe hours forging your resume. People gazing at your result take *10* to *15, 30* max, *seconds* to scan it.

"You have to grab a person's attention, and you only have about 5 or 10 minutes realistically to make an impact. The interviewer is thinking about everything . . . *except* you, when you walk in. So here's a focused list for having a productive session:

1. Focus on your *current* skills. They don't care what you did 10 or 15 years ago, particularly in the pre-Internet days.
2. Look for *bridges* from your former job or jobs. This would include also people from schools, industries, and experiences that can be vouched for by specific people. These are the bridges to new placement. But make sure that bridge can maintain that credibility, vouching for you if asked.
3. Know *specifically* what you bring to the party, and what your expertise is: accounting, chief financial officer, information technology, compliance. And frame your approach. As an example: 'There are three areas I can see myself [in] . . . advertising, market research and consulting.' These days in the job market you cannot have vague interests. And make *sure* the interviewer is clear when you leave.
4. Ask the source (the interviewer), if anything comes to mind in one of your three areas of interest. As an example, you might say you were interested in marketing either industrial or consumer. 'I got involved in this whole area of big data. Plays to my passion for research, which takes advantage of my digital analytical and info graphics capabilities. I know how to communicate with end users.' [This is a bit much, I say. But you have to show the source that you can walk the walk and can underscore what you do well.]
5. Assess the culture of the company. Look around you. It might be that most of the employees went to Notre Dame. See where you might fit in with this.
6. Ask what it takes to be successful in this organization. You may be surprised by the answer. And they will like the question.
7. Don't oversell. It can look desperate. Calm confidence . . . even if you're churning inside.
8. Overdress a bit.
9. Write a creative, original thank-you note. [I gave an informational meeting to a young man seven years ago, as a favor to one of my college roommates. The young man never sent me a

note. He can *not* come back to the well. If he calls again I'll tell him *why* he can't come back.]

10. *When* you get a job elsewhere, do a follow-up note telling the source where you landed; you never know in life when you need to come back."

This is advice from a premier search person. Here's my own take on being fired and what's next. I see dozens of young people a year, who either want to write or want to gouge themselves into the investment business. Employment is tricky. You never know what's going to intrigue a boss.

About a year ago, I was having dinner at a private club in Boston, quite a formal setting, in a place that was founded in the nineteenth century and has maintained high standards in a low-standard world. There was a young waiter there that night named Tom. He seemed to be floating through the evening, gracious to everyone but seeming like he was a member in disguise who decided to serve for the evening. At a quiet point in the dinner, he came over to our table. "I have your book," he said. "Do you think you could sign it for me?"

I was both flabbergasted and flattered. He told me that he really knew no one in business in our city. But that he really wanted to be somewhere, someday, in financial services.

"Tell me something; other than how different you appear to be in your physical approach to things, what sets you apart from others?" I asked.

He didn't skip a beat. "I skated a lot when I was a kid," he said. "My high school didn't have a hockey team. So I started one."

Tom is now in the training program in our office. He did the unusual. He separated himself from the average young person looking for a job. He distanced himself from the crowd and jumped out. That's what you have to do. Demonstrate that you can add value to the organization through hard work and that something special.

And, if you look back to Chapter 6. . .Tom grew up in New Jersey. True grit helps.

How are *you* going to jump out of a crowd?

**Have people who worked with you in the past step up
to the plate in enthusiastic ways, supporting your
future efforts.**

CHAPTER 21

PROVOCATIVE HEADINGS

Some days I get hundreds of e-mails. Don't assume, as many of you do, that your texts, e-mails, or tweets will be read anytime soon. Of the hundreds of e-mails I get, virtually none of them are business related, and almost none of them are spam. Most of them want something from me: advice, favors, or money. Many of these I delete automatically, trying to weed out the nonessential from the important. Some days there are so many that I can't face them and let them roll on, not looking. Often it is difficult to run a day-to-day business with so many intrusions popping up. And I think they do add to the feelings of anxiety I see in so many people. It occurs to me that other people, people I'm reaching out to, also have this problem. So I make sure that the subject or heading line is provocative and very different from the usual boring, vanilla subject that most people offer to you. I want people to read and answer my e-mail. If you are boring and unimaginative, I'm likely to never even open your message.

I know I harp on the theme of daring to be different. But how else do we differentiate ourselves from others so that they pay attention to us? We have to learn to approach life in ways that may be different from those of others and that make people smile or say, "Hmmm." For instance, one heading I use for e-mails is often "Your brilliant future." This makes people want to open my message, because the heading is something that surprises them. I *always* get fast answers from this heading, even from people who don't know me. Another one I've used with great success is, "Don't you miss high school?" It works because many people get lost in the past or obsess about it. It gets them every time.

If you want to be noticed in this country of more than 320 million people, you'll have to adopt some unusual measures. Subject lines on e-mails can sound so trivial. But with information overkill, you've got to cut through the fog.

**Even the smallest things in life need
a creative approach.**

CHAPTER 22

GETTING RICH: THE UPS AND DOWNS

For many years in the investment business, there were always dangerous moments when market movements were intense, when I could not keep up with what I had to do during a conventional workweek. Occasionally, I'd tell the family (my wife and three children) that I had to go into the office for a few hours on a Saturday or a Sunday. There was an underground parking garage for building employees. You can get a lot done in an empty office: no others to chat with, no phones ringing.

There might have been 200 underground spaces. On a Sunday, perhaps there would be 10 cars scattered on four levels. During the week the building was jammed with lawyers, investment office employees, consultants, and advertising agency employees.

I always noticed when I did my weekend overtime that every car in the garage was the most expensive, high-end, top-of-the-line vehicle there could be. Shining and standing tall. It underscored what my dad always told me. That "Life is *work*. Whether you want to hear it or not." And those working the hardest could have the most expensive toys.

If you want the good life for you and your family, there are trade-offs. One of them may be that you have to show up to work, when no one else is there. No one sees you. Except you. Because you're the one who has to make the donuts (which is what I call going to work).

Now, full disclosure: I had dinner with my entire family virtually every night until the kids fled the nest. I also exercised at a Y, a gym, or a club at least four times a week. I also have worked two full-time jobs, running money for people and writing books, for more than 50 years. I don't say this to pat myself on the back. These are choices we all make. A lot depends on what you really want in life. I hear a lot from young adults about their desire for work/life balance. What this will turn out to be in the real world, if you *want this* balance, is that you will almost never be able to set yourselves free economically. It's a sound bite not really grounded in reality.

I talk to lots of young people: young men, young women. I ask them, "What is your greatest fear for your future?" These people often are unmarried. The men tell me, "My biggest fear is that I won't find the right career path, and that I won't have the life that my parents had." The young unmarried women tell me, "I fear that I'll never find anyone to love me the way I want to be loved."

The one thing we cannot give our children is finding someone for them to love and be loved by in return. But fears of loneliness and isolation are part of our society becoming increasingly dependent on the virtual and not the real for experiences.

As for careers and work ethic, only you can have ambition and the fire in the belly. If it isn't in you now, it's something that is very difficult to learn. No one can really teach it to you.

There certainly are negatives to working your tails off and climbing various ladders to success. I was very lucky to have a mentor in the investment business who taught me how to make money for clients and myself. If I have any real net worth, I credit him, Sandy Weill, my true chairman for more than 25 years. But I was never in management, a dangerous, slippery slide on Wall Street, and almost *everywhere* else in corporate America. The corporation is like a court, where the king or the queen reigns. The courtiers hover around, sucking up, stabbing each other in the back, and jockeying for position. The politics are endless, and the journey up management ranks is so difficult. Virtually everyone who flitted about my chairman got divorced. He was a charismatic leader and he demanded total fealty from his courtiers. Almost universally, they chose the chairman over their wives and families. Trade-offs. You could get rich. But at what personal costs? One of the courtiers, a man I like and enjoy, was noted for coming into work before almost anyone else and being the last one out of the office. He would stand near the doors to the office early and give the hairy eyeball to anyone coming in after *he* did. He make an elaborate show of looking at his watch as people passed. He'd do the same thing as people left at the end of the day. This technique was designed to make people nervous, keep them on edge. And it did.

You can choose other paths. Simpler ones. But sooner or later, the biggest problem in the long run is money. Or rather, the lack of it. Trade-offs.

The extreme example here of work ethic is billionaires. I know a bunch of them, some for many years, going back to tag football on Sundays on a dirt playground, when all the guys who played were just out of college or graduate school, feeling their way into the future. Almost all billionaires I have known are unbelievably focused on the business of their career. They don't or didn't really care about you or anyone else, wives, children, or friends as much as they cared about the hunt.

What's the end of the classic film *Citizen Kane*? Kane, lost in grief for his childhood and what could have been. Or research the last days of billionaire Howard Hughes, looking like a madman, finger-nails 6 inches long, alone in his madness with his money. I suppose it's a case of "Be careful what you wish for." There are exceptions to this obsession with and focus on the prize at all costs. But I believe in knowing your characters. And regarding the billionaires, this assess-ment has nothing to do with how philanthropic they are.

This will help you understand the absurdities of life. And then understand what you're willing to give up to attain great wealth, or what you'll give up by having weekends off, to play and relax.

If you do get incredibly rich,
there are prices you will pay.
Sometimes accumulating riches leads to unhappiness
you never dreamed of.

CHAPTER 23

BRANDING: PULLING THE WAGON

We're all pulling the wagon at work in various ways every day, to put bread on the table and make our way in the world. Part of making our way has to involve an effort on all your parts to make yourself stand out a bit in a crowd. You're stuck endlessly in traffic; you're frustrated with the medical system; you smile knowingly when you see people with the push buttons on their desks that blurt out, "I'm surrounded by idiots."

Here are a few examples of how to brand yourself, how to get people's attention, no matter what your job. Years ago I had an idea for a book. It seemed at the time that we all faced a society that was too busy, was too cramped, and had declining standards in civility, with no one seeming to care enough. Sound familiar? This was in 1980. The book was called *Smart People,* and it was a guidepost to assembling your team of experts to care for you and your family in all the important areas of your lives. As I was writing the book, before a publisher bought it, two young people came into my life as clients, a young man and woman. They made enamel jewelry, small items in vibrant rainbow colors. One of the items was a heart-shaped pin. I started wearing one on my suit lapel, as a walking advertisement for them. It seemed accidental. But everywhere I went, people asked, "What's that pin?" The real answer took too long. So, after a while, I'd make up answers. "It's an award for love from the French government," or, "It's a lot cheaper than putting a flower in my lapel." But people asked about it everywhere. And it became the logo for my book *Smart People.* Bill Hamilton, the

New Yorker cartoonist, drew the cover. It shows a couple, a man and woman, being led to the front of the line at a busy restaurant. The man wears a heart pin on his lapel. This book you're reading is a lot about getting to the front of the line. The enamel heart pin became a brand, a way of getting the attention of others.

Years ago, I had a great shoe salesman for a client. It was in the days when shoe manufacturing was a huge industry in New England. His name was Bobby, and he was a walk-in, someone who just came into the brokerage office looking for someone to take orders from him. I was a rookie and the receptionist herded Bobby to me. The receptionist said to me, "He gave me Tootsie Rolls and said, 'Put me with a rookie who will care about me.'"

He was led to my desk in the boardroom, stuck out his hand, and said, "I'm Bobby the Tootsie Roll man and we're going to make beautiful music together."

Using the Tootsie Roll routine, he could get into the office of every chief executive officer he called on by charming the gatekeepers. Branding. Everyone, it seemed, loved Tootsie Rolls and remembered him.

My accountant collects all things penguin; for some reason, he loves penguins. "Why?" I asked.

"They're cute," he told me. But you cannot miss the point when you sit in his office: stuffed penguins, penguin stationery, and watercolors, oils, and pen-and-ink artwork of penguins on the wall. "It may seem sappy," he told me. "But whenever my clients see any image of a penguin, they think of me." Branding. He separates himself with this bird. People see him as someone who will care about them rather than as a simple pencil pusher. His brand humanizes his image and it draws clients to him.

This is a concept you should take to heart, because it's universal. Separating yourselves from the crowd is something you can do in virtually every business, in every profession.

Yes, you can view it as a gimmick. But if you believe that you're good at what you do, then figure out a way to bring 'em in the door. Then you can strut your stuff.

I know a barber named Karyn, excellent at what she does. But she brings street smarts into her customers' lives, which sets her apart from most of the other stylists, who work to make you feel better about yourselves. Barbers and bartenders are usually good at listening and schmoozing: therapists without couches. Karyn works in a college town, her shop surrounded by restaurants, tailors, and shopping opportunities of all kinds. She said, "I wander into the shops and restaurants and introduce myself to the owners, salespeople, the waitstaff, and managers. I'll give them my card and ask for theirs. And I tell them, 'I'll pay your bills, if you'll pay mine.' I give a lot of people introductory haircuts on the cheap to show them how good I am. Then they're hooked. They send customers to me and I refer business to them. I have a file of 1,000 business cards, assorted by category. I can't tell you how many people whose lives I've changed. And they add so much to my life, right back. Occasionally, I'll hang out near classrooms where freshmen go to lectures. I'll pass out my cards to them and chat. They'll come into the shop and I've got 'em for four years, plus their friends."

For my money, Karyn could teach professors at Harvard Business School a lot about marketing. And branding.

No matter whom you work for, try to brand yourself in ways that people will remember.

CHAPTER 24

TRIBES

We are still a tribal nation, despite more than 235 years as an independent country. I live in Boston, a distinctly tribal town. The tribes mostly hover together, with crossover on the business front. But socially, the tribes still trust their own more than they do the other tribes. A small asterisk for you readers of different cities in America. Boston is really all about three things: sports, politics, and revenge. Newcomers are very surprised by this, particularly the revenge side. I tell them, "Okay, we're at a cocktail party, all Boston people. See those two guys over there? They hate those other two guys near the bar. From the sixth grade on. They wish each other ill and they harbor grudges. It's what makes Boston so interesting."

No matter how gregarious and friendly you are, no matter how sensitive and inclusive you feel, it is natural to be most comfortable within your own tribe. Tribes can break down a bit beyond ethnicity. Hollywood people seem to be comfy only around other people in show business. Really rich, successful people are happiest around others who have also reached a certain status. They need to validate each other. It's all a dance.

I wander into this area of tribalism so that you won't be surprised if you are hired by a company where you look around and find yourself confused after you've worked there for a while. There are companies that favor people who grew up in the Bronx or went to Penn State or Texas A&M. There are organizations that favor women, gays, or graduates of Stuyvesant High School in New York or New Trier Township High School in Illinois. It's your job to figure out whether there is a tribal situation at your company and how you can position yourself to be accepted.

Maybe if our presidents understood tribes, we'd be a lot better off as a country. Don't discount how important this can be.

Start thinking about tribes. It may help you figure out a lot of them.

CHAPTER 25

WEEKENDS

This is the shortest chapter in the book, but it can help you in dealing with all manner of situations you'll discover in your business life.

I find that the most successful people do not necessarily think of weekends as time off. There are times when you will have to speak to colleagues or clients, or customers, even on a Saturday or Sunday.

Here's a rule you should know: never call people over 60 years old on a Saturday or Sunday between the hours of 3 to 5 PM. They likely may be napping and it will only piss them off.

Pay attention to nap time.

CHAPTER 26

BEING AN ENTREPRENEUR: WHAT IT TAKES

I've never been an entrepreneur. It was enough for me to have worked two full-time jobs my entire working life: running a money management practice, always under the umbrella of large investment banking firms, and having a creative life, writing books, and for magazines and newspapers, for almost 50 years. But I've bet my money on entrepreneurs, trying to learn something in the process, and perhaps add to my own net worth based on those bets. I do not believe in investing money based on friendship. But I do believe in betting on smart people first. If they happen to be friends, fine—but it's their brainpower I'm staking my money on, not the golf course relationships or the trip together to Burgundy. I like to bet on proven winners.

That guarantees nothing, by the way.

Webster's Third New International Dictionary's definition of *entrepreneur* says, "One who organizes, owns, manages, and assumes the risk of a business." It also mentions "The Yankee entrepreneur who descended on the desolated south to make his fortune." I like *both* of those definitions.

What separates entrepreneurs from most people is that they're not afraid to borrow money, they're definitely interested in other people's money (OPM), and they're not afraid of going broke, not even afraid of going broke multiple times. Because they all share the common feeling that the next one is going to be the big one. Their passion is convincing and real. They believe that their idea can and will set them free. And that their success will set *you* free, too, if only you'll back their play.

Good ideas are a dime a dozen. But who's going to put in the grunt work to bring the ideas to fruition? That's the key.

About 20 years ago I met Robert Sprung. He called me out of the blue to ask my advice. He was starting a company and said that he needed my help. "How'd you find me?" I asked.

"Oh, you're in the wind," he said. "An unusual answer," I thought. But it got my attention and was intriguing enough for me to make an appointment for Robert to come in and chat. I don't like to speak in hyperbole unless it's about Ted Williams or Caravaggio, or Emily Dickinson, but Robert Sprung was a different kind of guy. First off, he was brilliant, with a sense of humor on a high plane; was endlessly curious about ideas and the world; and was grounded by his youth and the strong values of Scranton, Pennsylvania.

Robert graduated summa cum laude from Harvard and won a Marshall Scholarship to Cambridge. In college he majored in the classics, Latin and Greek, and gave the annual Latin oration at Harvard commencement, traditionally both bawdy and hysterical—for the relatively few in the throng who understood Latin subtlety.

His charm and intellect sucked me in. Was he to be a professor? Way too easy. He wanted to make money.

His idea was built on globalization. "The world is exploding in new and exciting ways," he reasoned. "Corporations are going to need translations accurately done for everything: annual reports, memos, you name it. And I'm going to supply the translators *and* the translations."

Remember, anything that appears simple to outsiders *never* is simple. Sprung started his company, Harvard Translations, and hired the talent among the rich pool in Cambridge, Massachusetts: graduate students, scholars, a ready-made supply of workers.

He grew the company he founded. It thrived and he sold it to a public software corporation. He moved to Manhattan and started a branding company with a translation component and recently sold that to another public company on the New York Stock Exchange.

He and his family now live in Paris: Robert; his wife, Yuko; and their two young girls. They want the children to be multilingual, to know what it's like to be immersed in other cultures, and to learn to adapt and thrive.

I asked him to write down a few of his rules for being an entrepreneur: what has worked for him, and might work for you.

But remember, when you look at the world, and your futures, there are a million ways to the truth.

Here are Robert's rules:

I have a few words of advice for one species of entrepreneur—the one with a classic liberal-arts background, who envisions starting a business which is driven by ideas and which doesn't require lots of capital. Because this is the area, *mirabile dictu* [amazing to say], where I've had reasonable success. And in today's freelance economy, there are more chances for success than ever in this type of start-up.

Armed with the dubious weapons of classics degrees from Harvard and Cambridge—with a Latin oration at commencement thrown into the bargain—I would hardly be the type a VC [venture capitalist] would invest in. But I was fortunate enough to start a series of language-related companies, two of which were sold to public entities.

What advice on entrepreneurship do I dare mete out to liberal-arts types like myself?

1. *Festina lente* ("Make haste prudently"). Forget the business plan. I've seen countless *soi-disant* [so-called] entrepreneurs invest months in research, spreadsheets, and PowerPoints. Rather, have a plan that fits on two pages that your grandmother could understand. Then proceed immediately to point 2.
2. Sell something—anything! Get out there and sell your service and collect the money; get a client who will sing your praises, and don't care too much about the margin you make. If you can do this, you'll have validation that someone in the world actually wants what you think they'll need. The rest is commentary, as they say.

3. Start young. It's true that it gets harder the older you get. Some people fancy the *idea* of being an entrepreneur, but lack the stomach for it if starting too late, or simply can't afford the risk. You will probably fail a few times, which the true entrepreneur always seems to power through. If you can't imagine yourself failing, picking yourself up, and running at it again, look elsewhere.

4. *Verbum sat sapienti* ("a word to the wise")—take advice, but only from successful entrepreneurs. If you're any good, you'll find yourself surrounded by those willing to lend counsel. Business schools are filled with professors of entrepreneurship who've never done it successfully themselves. Avoid these like Charybdis and Scylla.

5. Study accounting. The course I took at Harvard Extension School turned out to be indispensable. And I don't mean finance or economics—I mean reading income statements and balance sheets. You'll be more effective in dealing with financial people (people never fully trust those they think aren't watching the pennies), and be more credible with eventual partners and acquirers.

6. *Respice finem* ("Keep an eye on the end")—start by keeping an eye on the exit! I've worked in an industry filled with very smart people—but many never considered an exit strategy until it was far too late. And there's no comparison in the amount of money you'll take off the table (to say nothing of the difference in long-term capital gains rates). Decisions you make in the very early days can lead logically to an exit, or may ultimately bar the door.

7. Finally, *Nosce te ipsum* ("Know thyself"). Ask yourself *why* you're doing it: if your knee-jerk answer is "because I'm driven to," you're probably an entrepreneur. If you're out of a job and see no other alternative, or you think you'll simply make more money this way, and you think you'll make a good entrepreneur—*dis aliter visum* ("it appears the gods think otherwise").

I had dinner this week with an old friend who has been a serial entrepreneur all his adult life. He calls himself Fenway Mike and attends most Red Sox games from his seats along the first base line.

He watches the games. But he mostly shoots the breeze with people around him, always teaching, always learning.

Fenway Mike went to the University of Pennsylvania, focusing on business studies. Getting out of school, he entered a family business in auto parts, a basic American business that many of you might think boring. But nothing is boring if you grow it, nurture it, and build into something special. Which he did. A friend from Penn later introduced him to ITT Corporation. "ITT bought my company," Mike told me, "technically setting me free to play golf and take my ease. But if you have the itch to create something," he went on, "you will *never* lose that itch. It will drive you on forever, *if* you're lucky."

Here's where mentors come in and show how important they can be to your lives. I'm not seeing this enough in the investment business. Or in media: newspapers, television, and publishing. Or in law firms. Too much disruption, regulation, bureaucracy, dumbing down, plain vanilla, covering of one's tail, and dismissal of the older employees with experience and an institutional memory. Too much virtual and not enough actual.

Mike was lucky that he picked up a few mentors after he sold his company. "My mantra," Mike said, "ever since I was smart enough to articulate it, became 'Energy and persistence conquer all things.'" He told me that this quote came from a line he learned when he was a freshman at Penn. They were the words of Ben Franklin, one of America's founding fathers.

Mike learned early in that merger the reality of large corporations laden with bureaucracy and levels of people. "ITT told me that the first year with them would be the honeymoon. The second year, they'd tell me what they wanted me to do. And the third year they'd decide if they wanted to keep or fire me."

Mike told me that ITT also gave him psychological testing before they bought his company. Mike was involved in the Young Presidents' Organization, YPO. There he met another tester who did counseling for them and convinced Mike, after evaluating him, that he might pursue public service, that his profile indicated that he wanted to help others. This led to his enrolling at the John F. Kennedy School of Government at Harvard. And it changed his life.

"Your brain never sleeps," Mike said. "The ITT experience convinced me that I always wanted to create something new, not be limited by the oppressive size of a major corporate structure. I remember at one early ITT meeting, standing at a urinal next to a corporate vice president. I asked him how he managed to stay so long in the company. 'I got news for you, kid. Here's how you can tell how you're doing. If you don't get ulcers or a heart attack, you're not committed enough to the cause,' and I've never forgotten that 'wisdom from the urinal.' He convinced me to try to make it on my own."

He went on. "At the Kennedy School, another mentor popped up, John Dunlop, who had been the secretary of labor for President Gerald Ford. He was a longtime professor and dean at Harvard, and probably the most influential figure in America on labor relations. Dunlop made me think about social entrepreneurship. He said to me, 'I want you to think about our country and how you can help transform it.'

"So I thought, because I was immersed then in something I hadn't thought about in years . . . *school*," Mike said. "So I asked Dunlop, 'How come we have *big pharma* but not *big education*?' And that became my 'bingo' idea."

Fenway Mike got out of the Kennedy School as a senior fellow, with new energy and a Rolodex loaded with names in the education field, and he started Eduventures, virtually the first company in the country to focus on consulting and research in education. It now serves as a clearinghouse.

Today Fenway Mike is a senior advisor to one of the most successful consulting firms in America. His role now specializes in advising entrepreneurs and researching the education markets. He is in his seventies now, on probably his fifth midlife crisis. Because he believes he is in midlife, living in the center of a city, with action and ideas around him. "I hope," he said, "that the young people I see in their twenties and thirties and early forties have many midlife crises as well. All of them can use these crises as springboards too. Because the fountain of youth is really positive attitude, and the eternal thought that 'If this one doesn't work, we'll get 'em the next time.'"

I have to point out to you that there is a downside to the life of the entrepreneur, be you woman or man. Success in America often comes with problems in relationships. One of the saddest refrains I've heard many times comes from divorced men, who have told me, "I never really knew my children from the first marriage. I was never home."

This is even more of a problem for your generation, where there are no defined roles in most marriages. Everyone basically is supposed to be doing everything.

So, go out there and thrive. But understand the potential downsides to almost everything you do. Like the Boy Scouts' old motto, "Be prepared."

This caveat aside, Fenway Mike has one of the happiest marriages of anyone I know. And it's his first.

Energy and persistence conquer all things.

PART II

BECOMING
FINANCIALLY SECURE

CHAPTER 27

INTEREST RATES

Whatever you do in life, interest rates will affect many of your decisions. Are mortgage rates going up or down? Can you get a decent yield on treasuries, certificates of deposit (CDs), or money funds? Will stock markets reward you based on interest rates? Do credit cards charge too much?

Predictions about fluctuating rates and their future take up enormous space in the financial media. The experts pontificate and pronounce. Talking heads, background noise, all geared to yesterday and tomorrow, all short-term thinking.

People will talk to you about interest rates and their direction all of your adult lives. Here's a true story that I believe should be taken to heart and remembered well when the subject arises.

One of the earliest venture capitalists was the New Yorker Fred Adler, a man of very strong opinions who did not suffer anyone he deemed a fool. And he shot from the hip. Adler was a force behind companies such as Data General, an early technology powerhouse; Staples, the office superstore; and many others. At the height of his career, one day, he assembled in his conference room a group of chief executive officers (CEOs) from business, government, and finance. One of them raised the subject of interest rates for important discussion. Before this began Adler had called for a telephone to be brought into the conference room, much to the annoyance of everyone there. Adler held his hand up to the room as if to say, "Stop the chatter." They watched, listened, and heard him say into the phone, "Ms. Buchanan (not her real name), do you know where interest rates are going over the next year? Uh–huh. Yup. Thanks very much." Adler hung up and addressed the bank presidents and the other CEOs.

"Ms. Buchanan is my assistant," he said. "She says she has no idea where interest rates are going in the next year . . . and neither do any of you morons."

I agree that virtually no one can predict rate swings with any consistent accuracy. Just like the world has been going to hell for thousands of years according to countless doomsday predictors. And we're still muddling through.

I remember college days late at night in dorm rooms, debating the cosmic subjects: free will versus determinism, whether Judaism is a race or a religion, and lots of other opinions, neither side convincing the other. Discussions of interest rates are like late-night ramblings in college. Time would be much better spent making a short list for yourself noting three things to do with your money when rates are low (3 percent or lower). And three things to do with your money when rates are higher than 3 percent.

It's not the highs and lows but rather what is in your strategy in both cases, how you prepare.

Rates will fluctuate. Have a plan for either case.

CHAPTER 28

INSIDER TRADING

There are several exercises I used and have used for a long time to help guide my investment decisions. One of them involves legal insider trading, not the kind that can send you to jail, like Martha Stewart, but the kind that has made me money legally over the years, and can do the same for you.

Every week in various media outlets, and on many Internet sites, lists are published, mandated by the Securities and Exchange Commission, of all the buying and selling by corporate insiders, officers, and directors of their company shares. The transactions cover number of shares and price range. And dollar amount. These corporate insiders must get legal prior approval to buy or sell these shares. Then they have to register these intents with the appropriate regulatory agencies. Once approval has been obtained, these insiders are given a narrow window, usually a few days, to execute these orders. Then, within days, the trades are published as public information, and general investors may use this knowledge (or not) to do their own trading.

This is an old technique for money managers, not unique. But, in my view, it's a technique generally unknown to the investing public. Here's how I use a strategy in relation to public insider transactions.

You might think that *selling* activity by insiders means that you should dump shares in the company. Not necessarily. Often, retirement and estate planning dictate insider selling. Lawyers and so-called financial planners tell their clients, "You have *way* too much invested in your own company. This is imprudent. You should start diversifying out of your company stock and not be so concentrated." This is often bad advice, because concentration in the right places is what really creates net worth, creates wealth. So insider selling can be misleading, not necessarily a sign that the public should sell the stock. It can mean only that the particular insider is being advised to diversify his or her holdings, spreading the risk.

On the other hand, insider *buying* indicates that officers or directors of corporations may find shares in their companies as the best place to put their own money. Can insiders be wrong in their judgments, too optimistic? Absolutely. Chief executive officers (CEOs) often praise their companies and their own management in wishful thinking, hoping their plans come true, while perhaps worrying that they may be very wrong. I was at a holiday party years ago at a neighbor's house. The neighbor was CEO of a big-board medical company. His stock in the previous year had taken a big tumble and was selling at that point for around $30. Being careful about asking specific questions, such as about potential earnings, I said, "I know things have been tough lately, how do you see the future about five years out?"

The CEO had had a few cups of holiday cheer. He said to me, his face red, "We are a $60 stock selling at $30. What does *that* tell you?"

Hmmm. It told me the stock in his view was cheap at $30. But this was on the way down to *$5* over the next few years.

But there were no insider purchases for them announced in the trade journals, and *those* are what I pay attention to. Often the reports of buys in a stock are in the millions of dollars. I will then, after reading the reports, do some due diligence on the companies, bringing my own research into the mix.

I love to own stocks where insiders are all sizable owners, eating their own cooking, so to speak. You all can check out various sites that track insider buying and often buy for yourself at prices cheaper than where CEOs have loaded up for themselves. I think it's a wonderful tool for following people who actually committed their own funds to something that you might buy for yourself.

This method is not foolproof, but I have found it very useful and profitable over the years. And even if you're Internet challenged, you can track insider activity weekly in the *Wall Street Journal* and *Barron's* and play the game with the big guys.

Track what corporate buyers are buying for themselves.

CHAPTER 29

DO YOU WANT TO MAKE MONEY, OR WOULD YOU RATHER FOOL AROUND?

In overseeing your own investments, know that there is no one way to profits. There are many ways and different opportunities: real estate, commodities, and collectibles, such as art or porcelain. The ways all demand many approaches. But the internal lesson in investing in anything is this: short-term traders, in my long experience, sooner or later miss the big buck. They miss the big score that only holding for the long term can give you. And what's more, I have never seen a short-term trader, in and out, who did not eventually blow himself or herself up—go broke. But it is in many people's nature to want to speculate, to want to place a few bets for the hell of it. This is why casinos are in business and why gambling is as old as time.

When people open brokerage accounts they are always asked about their risk tolerance. And almost everyone checks the box that says *conservative*. Then people call and say, "Conservative, really conservative. I'm risk averse before anything else."

One client of mine was a leading authority on taxes. He traveled all over the world solving tax issues for corporations and governments. About a month ago he called me and said, "I have a business suggestion."

"Sure," I answered.

"You should run a second portfolio choice, offer something with more action for people, something a little swinging. I'm just saying. . ."

"Okay," I said. "I'm a grown-up some of the time. What did you go and do?"

A little silence on the other end and then, "Well, I gave a little money to a young hotshot. He's all over various sites for traders on the Net and the little piece of cash I gave him is up about 40 percent in the last seven months."

"That's fabulous," I said. "Does he have a philosophy of investing?"

"Well," he said, "it's probably to 'make hay while the sun shines.' I'm trying to make this constructive, for you to fill a need in people to appeal to their nonboring side. Another tool in your toolbox."

There is an element in everyone to want to rebel against anyone telling us what is good for us. No one likes a scold, even if it really is for your own good.

In the Internet boom, companies with no earnings, and no dividends, were going public and soaring in price. Clients called my office and said, "John doesn't understand the new economy." Then 2000 arrived, the Internet bubble burst, and hundreds of public Internet companies collapsed into dust. During this time I kept asking people, "Do you want to make money, or would you rather fool around?"

Short-term trading and fads ultimately reward the person who takes your transaction orders. Not you.

I told my friend and client that I appreciated his business suggestion but that I believe one must focus on one's prime niche, and if it is working, don't stray from that formula. I would guarantee that if I offered a speculative portfolio for clients as an alternative to our main contrarian value style, it would not work. And it would confuse the existing client base, leading to people questioning my commitment, and moving themselves and their money elsewhere.

Certain professions are not suited to investing in the stock market. For instance, real estate developers hate stock markets. They love control and they mostly believe that *they* want to call the shots in the areas they know best. They cannot stand seeing daily fluctuations in stocks. They cannot get minute-to-minute price quotes on their properties, and the emotions of daily stock swings disturb them. I had a friend years ago who was a major real estate developer. In the end of the

1970s, he called me and said, "I'm sending you $500,000 to invest. Just do your thing."

"Fine. But you can't look at your account every day."

"I'll have lunch with you twice a year to check your temperature," he said. "That's it. Hands off. I'm not to look or be a pest."

The money came in and I started to invest slowly. *Two weeks* went by and my friend called and said, "I can't stand it. Cash me in."

Years later it was reported that he had lost millions investing with Bernie Madoff. Maybe there's a good reason to stick to what you know best: your own niche.

As for fooling around, there *is* a place for it in your own money life. What I suggest is that, whatever the sum you think you can invest, put about 10 percent of the amount in a separate account that you manage for yourself. This is your fooling around money, for you to experiment on your own. The only *real* way to teach yourself about investing is actually to put a few bucks on ideas, tips, or just flights of fancy. This is how you will teach yourself about profit and loss, and teach yourself to develop a sense for appearances and reality.

But a note of caution to the amateur stock picker—there are some who have very good ideas about stocks to buy. But I find that no amateur ever has a sense of how much to buy, or when to sell. An exit strategy is the mark of successful investors. Buying is the easy part.

And if you end up saying, "I'm no good at this," the losses will probably be minimal.

Hold a small piece of your own money out from professional managers to test yourself, trying your own ideas.

CHAPTER 30

DOING STOCK RESEARCH

Many of you work in large offices full of people. My own office is on two floors in a city high-rise building. We have more than 140 employees, and they range in age from 22 to 83, all of them consumers of lots of things. For some years if I wanted to do any market research, whether personal or for clients, I'd wander the halls and talk to people who work with me. On a personal note, I'll ask 25 people, different ages, about favorite TV shows. I got *The Sopranos, Breaking Bad,* and the early *Glee* from this source. I've also gotten best farmers' markets, best picture framers, the best hospital gift shop, and the best place to buy special honey. I believe in face-to-face opinions from people I know and have built up trust in from hours of shooting the breeze about the stuff of life. Websites are anonymous; searching is quick but opinions are so random. Boots on the ground are my greatest source of intel. And I have recourse if their ideas prove wrong. I can see them in person. Nobody likes a bum steer, or to be told in person that your honey tastes a bit like bear.

As for making money in the stock market, one of my prejudices in picking companies to invest in is finding those companies with strong balance sheets and debt that is relatively small or controllable, companies that cannot be squeezed when tough times arrive. Because they always do arrive. When they do, I want the companies I own not to be over leveraged. This means having too much debt.

On a personal basis there is something you must remember, the same way corporations must pay attention. If you owe too much money, on credit cards, your mortgage, or home equity loans, and you are forced to sell assets to pay your bills, this will be true: if you are forced to sell *anything*—real estate, stocks, jewelry, or art—to raise cash, some rule says that, if you're forced to sell, you'll always get a horrible price. So company debt is something I look at. But my number one interest in my office wanderings is about what the consumer is buying.

I usually get the germ of an idea from my coworkers, such as the public's use of Arm & Hammer baking soda. I was wheeling in a small refrigerator for my office when a sales assistant wandered by and said, "Make sure you get a box of Arm & Hammer baking soda and put it on a shelf. It will keep it smelling fresh." I took the idea to several dozen people on the two floors of my office. You'd be surprised at how many products and services you use are connected to companies that are publicly traded and that you can buy for yourselves.

I talked with about 30 people in my office, men and women, old and young. Ninety percent of them used Arm & Hammer products in their lives, from inside their refrigerators, to rubbing down furniture, to pouring some into their bathtubs while they lowered themselves into the warmth. "It's a godsend in my tub, for my body," one woman told me. "It's good for all my parts." That line was more valuable to me than any Wall Street analyst's report. People trusted the brand. Arm & Hammer has been a wonderful stock for years, something they trust and that millions of people use.

Some time later, someone smart in my life, not an insider, said to me, "Don't laugh. I think Tampax is a company ripe to be taken over by someone at a fancy price."

I told my wife about this, and she said, "Women talk to each other about all kinds of things like this. Some of these things we don't really talk about because they seem to be a given, like Tampax." One of my assistants went into the ladies' restroom and taped a note over the sink area. It said, "For market research, no names. How many of you use Tampax products? Just make a check mark." I left it up for two days. Then my assistant retrieved the sheet. Thirty-five women had checked *Tampax*. Two had checked *other*.

Have any of you ever taken the time to complete phone surveys? I haven't. I trust the public much more than I trust research reports. Eventually Procter & Gamble acquired Tampax at a premium price.

And we posted another sheet in the ladies' room, thanking all the anonymous participants.

You can do the same in the places you work, building your own networks of people you trust. And, in the workplace, make sure if you're doing this kind of down and dirty research that you ask questions of both men *and* women, old and young; spread it all around.

Lately, I've been wandering the halls, asking people for their anecdotal evidence of the success (or lack thereof) of Obamacare. I can't bet on anecdotal evidence like a stock. But it takes the temperature of America, which influences markets, up and down. And teaches lessons.

Use the people in your office for market research.

CHAPTER 31

MAKE LONG-TERM MONEY WITH SIMPLE THEMES

From age 10 on, it seems to me everyone wants to complicate our lives, not simplify them.

There are endless ways to analyze the stock market, its trends, fads, and individual companies. My own style is to be a contrarian, to go against popular sentiment. Then, when I identify areas I think are undervalued and unappreciated, I tend to move into them aggressively. This means *overweighting* the groups I like. For instance, on a mythical $1 million portfolio, if I like health-care stocks, I could buy two stocks that might make up 20 percent of the portfolio, or $100,000 in each of two companies. This strategy is risky, and I feel that I'm basically a conservative investor. But I like to be aggressive in places where I feel the downside is limited. There's the *simplicity* side of this contrarian-themed strategy, told with three examples:

1. In the late nineties, oil was selling at approximately $20 a barrel, and energy stocks were seriously out of favor. I depend a lot on smart friends and clients all over the world who do research for me. I pay little attention to most Wall Street analysts, preferring my own feet-on-the-ground perspective. You can do this, too, and again, it all comes down to relationships.

You will, as your business lives expand, have new friendships with people in different fields. You will also have your old friends and classmates from kindergarten on, who go out into the world and develop expertise in endless areas of which you have little or no knowledge. These people can be your guides into new fields and be your best analysts. Even better than arm's length research people, you will have personal relationships with these sources. There was a boy in my homeroom, freshman year in high school. Like most of us he was totally unformed, squishy, unsure of himself socially. But he was considered a brain, not in with any so-called in crowd. In high school the brains then were considered a bit strange. His parents and the brain moved to another town the next year, and I forgot about him. Today he's a billionaire, arguably the best hedge fund manager in history. This is the brain's revenge. He probably would not return my calls today in the era when the brains rule.

My source in energy matters came from someone who reached out to me after an article I had written for the *Atlantic* appeared. He became a friend. Frank had been an investment banker before he started an energy company in Billings, Montana. In the late 1990s, when oil was selling for around $20 a barrel, he was the first person who talked to me about potential global demand for energy, particularly from India and China. It wasn't just statistics. It was his painting pictures to me in words about the people of the world in emerging nations, increasingly connected by the Internet, who all wanted the good life, consumer goods, things, and . . . stuff of all kinds. That was a simple theme and I began buying energy companies for clients and *myself*. I still own more than a dozen energy companies, with strong long-term gains in all of them. In addition to the growth factor, most of the energy companies paid dividends comparable to 10- or 30-year treasuries. I love dividends. They sweeten the pot.

But the simple theme for energy was 7 billion people on the planet. They will want heat, light, and the good life. Which means they will be consumers of energy, fossil fuels. And I have to deal in reality, not dreams of a perfect world, of alternatives that may be years away from economic viability. This theme developed for me in the end of the 1990s, when wind and solar power were not on too many radars. Neither were oil and gas, out of favor at the time, and I had dozens of those companies, well established, to choose from.

2. More recently, another major theme of mine, as simple as the energy story years ago, was large pharmaceutical companies. We started to buy this group in 2008 on one seemingly easy-to-grasp idea: the demographics of America and the world. It applied the energy story to a different area. With more than 320 million Americans and 7 billion people on the planet, no one you and I know will ever be taking *fewer* pills than they are now. And we are starting to export our maladies, such as obesity and diabetes. In 2010, it seemed to me, the pharma companies, with enormous cash flow, paying dividends equal to or greater than 10- to 30-year treasuries, were compelling.

   Simple. I don't have to look at charts or listen to talking heads on TV. Common sense can give you investment themes, if you pay attention to the world around you.

3. One last simple theme to underscore this lesson. After the meltdown of the financial system, which began in the fall of 2007 and bottomed in the spring of 2009, virtually all sectors of the market were hammered in what was viewed as the worst market collapse since the Great Depression, which started in 1929. And for someone in the eye of the storm, managing money for several thousand clients, it *was* the worst collapse in my 50 years in this profession.

   In the chaos around me I thought *if* we survived as a nation with a viable economy, will there ever be deals again, or mergers and acquisitions? My answer was, of course, there *will* be deals, and there *will* be mergers. Venture capital *will* flow to new companies and ideas. Now, if the average citizen wants to participate in this activity, the price of entry is way too high to play in this sandbox. Private equity companies want to see from their investors $10 to $25 million to be included. Yes, there are the so-called funds of funds, which pool relatively small amounts into a pot that can spread small investments into a variety of these programs. In my opinion, I don't care for this approach: too many fees, too illiquid, and too long a time horizon. But you can buy shares in a few public companies that are the largest deal makers. I chose Blackstone as my vehicle for this simple theme. I liked its management, and its position in its niche, and if there *ever* were deals again, it would get its share. It also received evergreen income from the funds it managed, evergreen, every quarter. I like betting with smart people, and if you buy a stock as opposed to a closed partnership interest, you're totally liquid. If you're not happy, you can get out overnight, win, lose, or draw. You're *not* locked in. I began buying Blackstone for clients and myself at approximately $15.00 or less. The price is now $34, and there have been annual cash distributions as well since we began accumulating our position.

Simple things, if you're a contrarian, often take time to develop, and you should continuously try to shoot holes in your thinking and actually question, "Are my assumptions still valid?"

When the public seems to have discovered your theme, and your early brainwork is vindicated, *then* it is time to start slowly exiting those stocks and looking for what's next! Let the people who are late for the game get in last.

**All your investments should pass the
test of common sense.**

CHAPTER 32

CAN YOU DO IT YOURSELF?

Almost all of you are digital-age savvy. Many of you, I hope, have 401(k) plans and even investment accounts in addition to your company's retirement plan offerings.

There are today, a bewildering array of opportunities for advice on investing. But more and more there seems to be a trend toward simple, low-cost index funds that reflect various stock averages. These are plain vanilla investments designed to mirror market movements; they are liquid, and eliminate the need for human advice and counsel in the buying of individual stocks and mutual funds.

Warren Buffett, the legendary investor, dispenses wisdom and common sense wherever he goes. He has a cult following, in my view not just because he has an outstanding investment record but also because of his wisdom, experience, and counsel. In a country with an increasingly anonymous population lacking in these qualities, people are desperate for good old-fashioned advice, given by someone so fatherly and wise like old-time headmasters and educators, people who more and more seem to be missing from our lives. Buffett has revealed that his will calls for his assets to be allocated 10 percent into U.S. Treasury securities, 90 percent into index funds, low cost and merely investing in the averages, funds with no active management by others. In his lifetime, he manages his own money, trusting only himself with the task. Clearly, he really does not ever rely on anyone ever being as astute as he, when he goes eventually to that great Exchange in the sky.

Most of my readers are young, with decades more to live and make many decisions for themselves, and their families. Maybe you enjoy making money and investment decisions yourself. And many of you have already chosen index funds to point you in the right directions. I find an overwhelming desire on the part of the public to have real people guide them in the key areas: law, medical, and money matters. As you all get older, you suddenly will realize that you don't have the time to invest on your own. You need hands-on advice, not virtually, not by robots, but by real live smart people who consider the best interest of you and your family. Tough to find. But it can be priceless if you do.

My whole investment business has been built with this something extra. And the special sauce is the personal touch. Our business is the largest and most demanding it's ever been. We have a practical game plan. We do the investing ourselves, not farming it out to computer programs or outside managers.

In this age of the misinformation revolution, you can find hundreds if not thousands of answers to almost everything: medical diagnoses, secrets to financial success, and the meaning of life and God's goodness. Or not. You can indeed manage your own money, do your own will or divorce, and find the right drugs for your bursitis. But sooner or later you will need practical help and advice. And you'd better start working at your young ages at building your own team of real people you can summon to your side. Not technology but people who either show up in person to help you or give you a fast appointment to look in your eyes and help you with your problem. I tell people who are clients and friends, "If you are really in trouble, send up the Bat-Signal, and I'll respond as soon as I can." They remember the phrase from *Batman*. They use it judiciously. But they *do* use it.

Sooner or later you're going to need that personal touch, a real one, not a virtual one.

CHAPTER 33

GETTING TO PEACE OF MIND

When it comes to your money, sleeping through the night perhaps is more important than anything else, even more important to many people than seeing your money grow. One of our primary goals for our clients, particularly in this era of anxiety, is to get them to that sleeping point.

We all have had what I call the "Oh, my Gods," when we wake at 3 AM obsessed with certain demons that plague all of us: family, health issues, business fears, and relationships. We tell prospective clients, "Whatever you have night sweats about, we want to make sure, wherever possible, that it isn't about your money."

But it is *your* money, not your wealth manager's. We are all subject to irrational behavior, and I have to listen to my clients and give them the options. Their decisions may not be rational. They may even be stupid decisions, very much not in their own economic best interests.

Your job with your own money is to try to talk yourselves out of the stupid moves.

A dear friend of mine has kept seven figures in money funds for five years, more than 30 percent of his liquid assets. Fear of meltdown and the daily slog of terrible news has him in a frozen position, willing to accept virtually no income on his money funds. I recently gave him one last try, pointing out how much money he had cost himself in one of the best times in history to really create net worth.

"The point is that I can sleep nights, *not* worrying about the money I may have cost myself," he replied. Remember, peace of mind, your own *and* the client's, is what we search for. And sometimes the wrong moves in life, or inaction itself, can be an emotional cure. This often means more than a little more money does.

More money with *any* risk attached is not worth it to some people.

CHAPTER 34

PICKING SOMEONE TO WATCH OVER YOUR MONEY

A man from Connecticut once interviewed me about managing money for him. He really asked me only one question. "This is key," he said. "Why are manhole covers round?" I thought about this, quickly thinking, "I have no idea" and "Why is he asking me this?"

"I have no idea," I said.

"Aha," he said triumphantly. "There are actually *two* right answers. One is: manhole covers are round because if removed they can *never* fall into the hole. Number two: they're heavy and cumbersome, tough to carry for one person. But they can be *rolled* because they're round." He was an executive in a manufacturing company, making machine tool parts. "What I asked you was one of the questions Microsoft asks prospective employees. It tests their reactions to real life, evidently."

"I don't think we're going to be a good fit," I told him.

"Well," he said, "I kinda agree. You couldn't answer the question."

"The question and the answer," I said, "has absolutely nothing to do with managing money. Nothing."

We agreed to disagree. But after that I was determined to tell anyone who came to see me for the first time the *really* important questions you should ask anyone who wants to manage your money.

First of all, "What do you charge?" is the wrong question as well. Of course, you should ask what the manager charges. But down the line of importance. All reputable money managers are pretty close in their fee structure. Competition tends to ensure that. We try to price our services, for instance, to be in line with many no-load mutual funds. It's simple: zero to $500,000, $1\frac{1}{2}$ percent of assets, *no* transaction charges, (commissions); $500,000 to a million, $1\frac{1}{4}$ percent; and more than $1 million, 1 percent. Soup to nuts.

Here are the questions almost *no one* has ever asked me. And they are the key questions to ask anyone who presumes to guide you in money matters.

1. "What's your philosophy of investing, Ms. or Mr. Money Man-ager?" If the manager cannot articulate his or her philosophy in a few simple paragraphs, in *plain* English, then keep looking.
2. "What has been one of your greatest triumphs in the market? And what was the decision making that brought you to it? What did you learn from the process?" Then you ask, "What about one of your biggest mistakes? What went wrong and what did you learn from that mistake?"
3. "What do you own yourself? Where do you put your own money?"

My father used to tell me, "Don't count other people's money. You'll be wrong in *both* directions." I'm sure he was right. But I have a feeling that many people who wish to oversee *your* money do not have much net worth of their own. I would want a money manager of my choice to have skin in the game, to own what he or she is buying for *me*. If the manager can't answer the third question to your satisfaction, move on. I would want people watching over my money to be eating their own cooking.

**Ask the *right* questions when you interview
financial advisors.**

CHAPTER 35

WHEN YOU'RE FRIGHTENED BY THE NEWS

I had a client, long passed away, a woman I called "The Countess" because she was highly theatrical and seemed like an actress who could have played Catherine the Great. She'd dress expensively and make grand entrances into any room. She lived in Manhattan and had escape places in Cape Cod and Palm Beach. Her husband was a serial entrepreneur who had many ups and downs: very rich for patches of their long marriage, quite broke for different periods. Always confident that he could come back stronger than ever from the bumps.

During one low point, she said to him, "Harry, I'm scared."

"Where are you most scared?" he answered. "Palm Beach, Cape Cod, or Park Avenue?" She laughed when she told me that story.

For years I have written a quarterly memo to clients and friends: chatty comments about markets, trends, and where we're comfortable (or not) investing their money and our own. One of my themes for a long time has been, "Folks, the news is going to be terrible every day for the rest of your lives. But most of it will have *nothing* to do with your business or the effects on your own family. If you're in business for yourselves, you're not in a fetal position under the desk because of the headlines. You're doing your best to invent or reinvent yourselves, trying to beat the competition and bringing home a paycheck to feed your families."

Personal events can devastate us. The loss of people so dear and reversals that take nicks out of our treasure and our souls. My first employer, where almost all my liquid money was invested, went broke. Terrible management and terrible times, the early 1970s. My last company, Citibank, in which I had a considerable investment, went from $55 to less than a dollar in about a year's time. It was probably the best-known bank in the world, barely surviving in the financial meltdown of 2007 to 2009. Terrible management. Terrible economic times. I never really lost sleep over these personal events. What cost me sleep was planning: How do I overcome this? How do I refocus and come back? I believe in looking over chasms, on not dwelling on the past because that can suck the life out of you.

In simple terms the world has been going to hell for thousands of years, and in business or the stock market, scared money never wins. The news, the daily problems we face, distilling the latest threats to all of us, mostly disappear after a few weeks. But the daily threats are *always* replaced by the new virus, the new upheaval, and the new acts of violence. Concentrate on *you* and *your* productivity.

There are times to be selfish, and to screen out headlines that mostly have nothing to do with your own battles for survival and prosperity.

Screen out the news and concentrate on *you*.

PART III

BECOMING YOUR OWN PERSON

CHAPTER 36

_____

THE ACTOR AND THE ACTRESS

Some of you are married and some of you are divorced. Some have not experienced either of these conditions. But you can all benefit from this chapter.

Many of you know by now that marriage is tricky, as are all long-term relationships. Tricky, often wonderful, and tough to keep fresh and alive. I have written before that a sense of humor is the most important element in a successful marriage and that my father advised me to "marry funny, not money" as the key to getting along "through sickness and health, for richer or poorer," and all the other vows one takes. Of course we take those vows in a blur on the wedding day, when, to be honest, that day brings so many anxieties and otherworldly sensations that almost all brides and grooms bump through it as if it's unreal, happening to someone else. And in many ways, it *is* unreal.

I believe that to have a truly long marriage, one of the partners, the man or the woman, has to be a great actor or actress. You will spend more time with your spouse than anyone else in your lives, and during this time you all will be tempted to say things, in anger or lovemaking, even in all innocence, things that will be hurtful, harmful, and sometimes unforgivable to the other person. And once said, you can never put this genie back in the bottle. The phrases will haunt you and be hurled back to you at almost every stressful moment. As the actor or actress, you should be aware of the in-the-moment possibilities for doing lasting damage by what you blurt out.

The actor or the actress will set the tone for the marriage. If there is true caring at the root of the relationship, the ability to act a character in the play of your life will help keep things together.

If your friends read this and ask you, "Who's the actor in your marriage?" you should just smile and shake your head as if to say, "It's beyond me." It may keep you from uttering words you can never take back.

**There are some genies you cannot put
back in the bottle.**

CHAPTER 37

HAVING SOMETHING TO TRADE

We all feel insecure no matter what we achieve. Long before the word *dyslexia* was invented, I used to see numbers inverted, or upside down. I was allowed to leave second-year algebra in high school and take art instead. Yet I've been in the money management business for a lifetime. And my business, now at age 75, is bigger than it's ever been. Everyone I grew up with was terrible at something: sports, music class, rope climbing in gym, Latin, or physics. My high school accommodated me and let me concentrate on writing, reading, and drawing.

There was also a manual arts building that taught shop: electrical, carpentry, and plumbing. We called it the "nyuk nyuk" division, and yet most of those guys ended up being incredibly successful in life. Much more successful than anyone I knew who had been voted "most likely to succeed." One of these guys in nyuk nyuk eventually became the most successful plumber in the richest town in Massachusetts. He used to make my manual training projects in the eighth grade: the bird feeder and the cranberry picker/letter holder. And what he did with his money was to buy raw land in our town for eventual development. Reminded of the nyuk nyuk days, he just laughed. "We were the best jocks in the school," he'd say. He was right about that. "And we had the last laugh, too."

Being labeled in early life can be a destructive thing. I run my billion-dollar money management business that involves much more than just investments. It is long on advice and counsel in old-fashioned ways.

I would eventually swap financial ideas with my plumber classmate for his assistance with plumbing and contracting. When I was in the army, we had a number of recruits from Puerto Rico. They had been told before they came to the States by the gossips of their community that they would be attacked in their beds by the gringos. In basic training, they slept with their bayonets under their pillows. As the weeks went by, I began to kid with them and tell them in halting Spanglish stories about America, history, and South American friends of mine. They discovered I was horrible at making a tight bunk and cleaning my rifle properly. They worried about passing inspection, knowing I was inept at so much involving daily living. The tradeoff: they'd do chores for me as long as I'd tell them stories, and make them feel it was not so threatening up in North America.

You can all work around your deficiencies if you start to think more creatively about the areas in which you shine: technology, languages, writing or drawing, or music. Your special interests can be traded for help where you need it.

Ever deal with building contractors? No-shows? Cost overruns? Their subcontractors out on a bender? I have a contractor in my life who does everything for me, from building a small studio with seven different kinds of woods to changing filters in sinks and lightbulbs in 16-foot ceilings. No job too small. Why? Because I teach him life lessons in areas no one has ever spoken to him about, such as, "You can go anywhere in the world and be perfectly dressed for royalty or chief executive officers or a policeman's ball if you always travel with a classic blue blazer and two black turtlenecks: one wool, one cotton." He tried it at a client's cocktail party, one he was nervous about as being too fancy.

"It worked," he told me later, delighted with the results. "Everyone talked to me." He wants to know about places he has never visited, and strange people he has never known. I call this "bedtime stories for grown-ups": people love to hear stories that pique their own imaginations.

You can trade for almost anything if you use your own specialties. It is surprising how things such as dress tips can make a difference.

Figure out what you have to trade.

CHAPTER 38

THE 110 PERCENT RULE

I have a smart friend named Joe, who was in the business of commercial real estate, leasing and selling space. He is a people person, liking them, a fine salesman. At one point he had some commercial space he needed to sublet on the Boston waterfront. The space was advertised in the trade papers, long before the Internet. "Sublet deals are a pain," he told me, "but I was dealing with a guy who was relocating to Boston. He was representing a medical company, Germany based, growing their business in American markets."

Joe told me, "I knew he was relocating, and would probably need housing, so I gave him a little verbal tour of the Boston area towns, and recommended a realtor who was patient and nice. The man bought a home in one of these towns, particularly when he learned the quality of the public schools."

"My two girls play soccer and boy, would I love to be plugged into that in my new town," the client said. My friend Joe made a few calls and connected his client with the local soccer people.

"I'll never forget this," said the happy client.

Several years later, my friend had left his job in real estate and was searching for his next career, and he wanted something part-time. He tried calling the company he had done the sublease with and was told, "Sorry, we can't find a way to fit you into this organization." Joe persisted and was told that his qualifications would be passed up the ladder one more time but that he should not hold his breath.

Joe had long pushed away the memory of the man whom he had helped find a home. But the man was now, incredibly, the local boss who had received Joe's application. He called Joe.

"I've never forgotten the soccer league help you gave me. Both my daughters are doctors now. I'm waiving a lot of our part-time rules for you. You've got the job."

This job has given Joe a brand-new successful jolt for his later years. "And it's all because of me giving 110 percent of my efforts," he said. "If I give 120 percent it would've been too much. Like sucking up, planting the wrong message. But 110 percent . . . going a little extra I guess, planted a seed."

The most unexpected people have long memories. They remember hurts, and they remember kindness.

What you have to do is pay attention to others, not in an artificial way, nothing forced. You never know when this can come back and resonate. And most of it takes little or no effort.

In this regard, I have many stories about ways the 110 percent rule has worked for me. Do you know about TED Talks? These are filmed brief discussions, 18 minutes, from people distinguished in some way in technology, entertainment, or design: TED.

The talks, available on YouTube, are almost classroom presentations: concise, informative, and provocative. I received a call from a man who introduced himself as the prime mover in Boston to produce that city's first TED Talks, called TEDx. He invited me to participate in the first Boston rollout of the TED concept. "And we expect," he told me, "to have at least 2 million viewings of our talks."

"Thanks for including me," I told him. "I'm honored."

"Do you know why I called you? It's only partly because you have a new book on sale. It's because years ago you agreed to see me in your office, to give me a steer in the right directions. Me, a kid without a job, terrified about what would happen to me in life. You chatted with me. I expected some advice and you asked what dreams I had. One of the dreams involved a nonprofit organization, and you said you knew someone on the board. You also said, 'Let's call him now.' And you did. You made the call and eventually I was on that board as well. You went the extra mile for me and I've never forgotten it."

My TEDx talk has had several thousand viewers, and I know it has resulted in hundreds of my book copies sold. And it's still rolling. Now I know that unconsciously, I went that 110 percent. It will pay off for you as well, in ways you could never predict. You can watch that talk at www.TEDXBeaconStreet/JohnSpooner.

Generosity can pay off in ways you could never predict.

CHAPTER 39

LIFE LESSONS: DON'T LOOK BACK

You will be invited to special events that will involve travel that can be a pain in the neck and inconvenient. And you'll say no because it is inconvenient. Then you hear reports from people about how great the event was and how it should not have been missed. For years, I would take the lazy way out, refusing various invitations, preferring to stay home and not bother. When my wife, Susan, died, and travel became solo, I literally woke up one day and said, "Never look back on anything that sounds special and say, 'I should have gone to that concert,' 'I should have gone to that play-off game in Dallas,' or 'I should've gone on that theater tour in London with fellow nonprofit board members.'" Because going to pain-in-the-neck destinations can not only be illuminating but also change your lives in interesting ways.

In the last year I was invited to a black-tie dinner at the Hearst Castle in San Simeon, California, hosted by the Hearst family. This involved flying to San Francisco, driving or puddle jumping in a plane to a town near the destination, and renting a car there. To me, traveling 3,000 miles for a party is a pain in the neck, particularly when a 45-minute flight from San Francisco to San Luis Obispo turned into an 8-hour logistical nightmare. But I traveled with a man in his midforties who told me stories of his generation, the anxieties and fears about challenging times in careers and relationships, and his hopes for the future. These conversations alone were worth the trip.

William Randolph Hearst was a legend in American business. Hearst was the model for the Charles Foster Kane character in the classic Orson Welles movie *Citizen Kane*. The actual castle, particularly seen at night, in all its haunting splendor, surrounded by people in formal clothes, made me feel as if I had chewed on a magic mushroom and landed back in the 1920s, glamorous and decadent, too. Cocktails were served around the indoor pool, in shadow, all brilliant blue below the waterline, that looked as if Roman emperors had cavorted there. Later there was dinner in a baronial banquet hall, full of toasts, little dances around the long trestle table, and people, new to one another, making friends. I spent time with several of the original puppeteers with the Muppets, a late-night TV host, and the current namesake of the original press baron. William Randolph Hearst III wove tales for me of his family, California's stewardship of the castle, the current state of California politics, and the peculiar phenomenon of American cities San Francisco epitomized. And I would have missed it all if I'd taken the easy and comfortable way, staying at home.

Last winter I finally said yes to urgings of friends to visit them in Rome. Most of us can be lazy about traveling, particularly because this post 9/11 time, and financial meltdowns on top of it, make air travel often a nightmare of frustration. And, traveling alone after my wife died removed my rock from so much of what I did. She referred to herself as "Susan Spooner, senior cartographer," because she paid attention to everything, while I watched people and tried to imagine them melting into characters I could write about. I think I am afraid of depending on the lifelong knowledge that I'm a klutz, or depending on trusting the kindness of strangers. But I believed even more in not looking back and saying, "I should've gone to Rome."

So I did. My two friends, David and Judith Barrett, had immersed themselves in the language, history, food, wine, and people of Rome. They were my docents, my guides, and my personal shoppers, forcing me to try speaking Italian. Judith had written six great cookbooks and gave dinner parties for me in their apartment overlooking the Vatican. The husband had grown up in Brooklyn, a student of history and character, giving me so much trivia of the city that only a Brooklyn boy could give: funny and full of irony and observations that taught me more about Rome than any guidebook could ever provide. And when I returned to Boston, I had e-mails from two people I had met there. One of them, an expatriate for many years, decided she needed help managing her money and became a client with a seven-figure account.

The other person, a young woman from Turkey who was traveling through Europe going to operas, now swaps e-mails with me, full of wisdom about all things Turkish, and as a sidebar, special insights into the Middle East. Priceless.

Never turn down out-of-town adventures because you're too busy, or they're too much of a pain in the neck. Be curious, and be out there, interested in how other cultures exist or disappear. It can enrich you in ways you never could have predicted.

Squeeze the lemon dry.

Never look back and say, 'I should have gone.'

CHAPTER 40

GET YOUR ELDERS' STORIES

Do you know anything about your family's past, about your ancestors on both sides? Do you have any ideas about where some of your quirkiness comes from? Recently, there have been stories in the press about John Kerry's Jewish roots, facts that presumably the secretary of state never knew. Most of us wonder, from time to time, "Where did we come from? What propelled the family here? What secrets don't we know?" Sites such as www.ancestry.com are extremely popular. But the personal stories from the older generations are what sing to us, and teach us. Not only family history but also history about the lives and times of others around them.

People love to talk about themselves and their past. Even recluses and people who claim to be private can open up like clams if you ask the right questions. And once they start, they'll just keep rolling.

My grandfather was in the hospital several times in his later years. He lived until his early nineties, a tough immigrant, full of grit his entire life.

Asking him about his past made him forget any pain, forget that he was in a hospital room. He came to this country in 1893, and he told me, "The biggest difference between Europe and America, and it amazed me when it first happened, is that in America, when you got in a fight, the other guy always let you up." He talked to me often about his early days in America.

"As a greenhorn kid," he said, "full of wonder, I understood fast that you had to stick up for your rights. You couldn't let yourself be pushed around. That's why my father left Europe. He was a butcher. He could do nothing against the soldiers who would come into our little town, burn houses, stick swords into our beds, into our clothing, looking for money, jewelry, anything of value. In America I got into lots of fights. You had to fight because everything was centered on the corner where you'd hang out with your friends. My great-grandchildren watch television. They have everything, and they complain to me sometimes about having nothing to do. Boredom and self-pity are the two elements that will kill you faster than any disease. You'll be dead between the ears."

He spent most of his childhood on the streets of Boston's West End, in competition, playing games. He and his friends rolled hoops on the Boston Common, spun tops on the sidewalks, and swam in the Charles River.

"All of our entertainment was outside the home," Grandpa has told me. "Fruit and vegetable men would peddle their produce from carts. We would steal ice from the milk cart, and the milkman would chase us through alleys, over fences. He didn't care whether the milk soured or not. Our year was spent in contests: jumping, running, baseball, swimming, sneaking into burlesque shows. The show cost 10 cents for the gallery, but a dozen of us would come in and individually march by the ticket taker, telling him the next guy would pay for all. The last kid would pay a dime, but by then we would be all over the theater. At the burlesque it wasn't just stripping. It was variety shows, vaudeville. There I saw "Gentleman Jim" Corbett, who was the heavyweight champion. He would do a routine, punch a bag, jump rope, demonstrate his famous solar plexus punch.

"Just about that time a most wonderful thing happened. It was in 1904. They built a gym a few blocks from our house. It changed the life of the gang on the corner, because it meant we had a place to play inside all winter. And it was also a place to bathe. We all lived in apartment houses. My home was a four-room flat. My mother, my father, and I lived with my three brothers and sisters. There was one bathroom, and we all washed ourselves in the sink. We had a bathtub, but that was where we stored coal for our stove.

"Sports were part of us. We all played everything there was to play. I was a baseball catcher, the leader. Our team was The Hemlocks, from the West End, and we played every town or regional team around Boston. I boxed professionally also, under the name Kid Manning, at 130 pounds, on barges in the Charles River and in clubs in Cambridge, Boston, and Providence. That's what the gym taught me. For $15 a fight I'd go up against all the tough little guys who grew up just like me, whether they were Jewish, Italian, or Irish.

"And you got to remember, this was always in our spare time, when we weren't working. All the kids worked. I was a delivery boy for the butcher, a paper boy, I carried ice, I was an usher. Six days a week, after school and on Saturdays. It was life, everybody in the same boat. When I was getting married my wife made me stop fighting. It was marriage or boxing. I got married. But I never gave up the love of sports. Two years after our wedding, in 1912 it was, I was going to the store to buy some milk and bread on a Sunday morning. I was wearing a suit and tie and hat, like all the other Sunday strollers. At the corner there were all sorts of people gathered. As it happened, that was the starting line for a 15-mile race, a walking race. Walking was a big event then, the shuffling fast heel-and-toe event. I took off my hat, tie, and jacket and entered the race. It was 15 miles up Commonwealth Avenue and back to the starting point. In my street shoes, out of 70 participants, I finished third." As I write this, I'm looking at the pewter cup that he won.

My grandfather used to play catch with me until he was in his late eighties. He had a battered catcher's mitt from the 1920s that he would take every spring to the Boston Braves Florida training camp, where he'd pester the players to throw to him. After the Braves left for Milwaukee, he would take his glove and follow the Red Sox to Sarasota. He always threw a heavy ball and always aimed to hit me in the chest with his throw. The last time we played he could still throw a bigger curve than I could ever manage in my life.

The last time I saw him in the hospital, as I left, he flashed one finger at me, then two.

"What's that?" I asked him.

"Remember," he said to me, "one finger for a fastball, two for a curve."

I loved my grandfather and his stories brought history to life, far richer than anything that could be grabbed from the often-dull history books. And his stories gave me many lessons, the biggest of which was that we didn't just spring into our father's and mother's lives as a blank. We all have a past and a rich history in tales of where we came from, what made us, and how our forebears had triumphs and joy and sadness, just like we do.

Pay attention to these old people. They can help us stay young.

CHAPTER 41

DON'T BE A TRUSTEE OR AN EXECUTOR*

I put an asterisk after this chapter title because obviously professionals such as lawyers, or bankers, will serve in these roles. But my purpose in writing this book is to make my readers look at their lives in some unconventional ways, ways that might make things easier and smarter for you to avoid pitfalls you could never have anticipated.

I learned this lesson to avoid acting as a trustee or as an executor of anyone's estate early and the hard way. Unfortunately, the hard way is what teaches us the best. My parents had best friends in Chicago, a couple smart and successful, the husband in manufacturing, the wife in retail, focusing on women's fashion at the high end. The husband died and she eventually remarried. She had two daughters, both very different. One went into business, primarily real estate. The other you could call a hippie, living a nomadic life, having a child out of wedlock, and eventually becoming a midwife. Their mother asked me, she thought, to protect her daughters, whether I would act as executor of her will when she died. The real estate daughter would get her bequests outright; the midwife's money would be in trust, with me as the trustee. "Of course," I said. "My parents loved you guys. And I love you. It would be my pleasure to make sure your girls have peace of mind and security."

When you say yes to something that may be years away, you tend to push it into the future and out of your mind. But time rolls on quickly. The wonderful woman died. And suddenly there I was, executor and trustee. This estate was in Chicago. I'm in Boston. One girl is in

Germany, the other somewhere vague out West. "I'm screwed," I thought.

Most of us go into new experiences with goodwill, trusting most of the people we meet, anxious to be honest in our dealings, and mean what we say. Life has a way of beating these thoughts out of us. Dealing with the sisters was a disaster for me. The German woman wanted me to say a prayer for her mother in every room of her apartment. And I could never get her off the phone unless I pleaded an emergency in my family, or that my kidneys were about to burst if I couldn't hang up. The midwife sister resented her mother's decision not to give her the money outright. She had to go through me for any distributions. Therefore, she not only resented me. She also hated me.

And in promising their wonderful mother that I would serve as trustee and executor, I also told her that I would take *no compensation* for these roles. If any of you is foolish enough to take on duties like these, *do not ever* do this for free.

It didn't take long for the Germany sister to grab all the money in my care. At this point she claimed that she had forgotten English and spoke mostly to me, on crackling with static lines, in German, which I don't speak. The same year, on Christmas Eve, I got a special-delivery letter from a law firm, announcing that the midwife was suing me: to complicate this, the wonderful woman's estate lawyers were in New York. I was still in Boston. They had no stake in me; I barely knew them.

Wherever you wander in life, make sure wherever you can control it that you do not do business at arm's length. If you change your main residence to another state, find local practitioners who know the landscape. I felt helpless, determined to resign from my trusteeship. But the New York lawyers, to whom I was some stranger on the hook, told me that I couldn't resign unless we could find another trustee willing to take responsibility for the midwife. "Doomed," I thought. "Three hundred million Americans and I can't find one who will set me free." All of us go into panic mode from time to time; it's natural when we cannot see a way out. Who would want to be a trustee for such a difficult person?

By some miracle, San Francisco, a city that understands perhaps more than others how being a midwife would go hand in hand with having a platinum American Express card, provided a local trustee for her. The lawsuit was dismissed on all counts before this, and she disappeared from my life like a tumbleweed on the prairie. I had a sister-in-law who used to say to her husband when he would shake his fist against the sky, frustrated at something he had done . . . "It's your own damn fault, David." And it usually was. As it was my fault for reacting from the gut when asked to be an executor and trustee. There was no way I could foresee that most families are dysfunctional, all in their own ways. And I didn't really appreciate the instinctive desire for siblings to resent one another. And above all else, just to grab the money.

Do not accept executor or trustee roles if possible. And *never* do these jobs for free.

CHAPTER 42

BUYING AND SELLING JEWELRY

Many of you reading this have either bought or received an engagement ring.

Or you have bought jewelry as gifts for special people. Or you have inherited family heirlooms.

If you have bought jewelry, undoubtedly you have saved receipts that most likely have included the estimated value of the object. This is for all of you, like me, who are amateurs at this game. We know what looks pretty and we know our budgets.

My father took me to buy an engagement ring for Susan, who would be my fiancée and eventually my wife. I have a friend who calls adventures like this "nervous making." And it was. We went to the jewelers' building in our city to buy the ring wholesale, not retail. "Do you know what business Tiffany's is in?" my dad asked me.

"Sure," I said, "they're in the jewelry business."

"No, they're not," he said. "They're in the Blue Box business."

People have been brainwashed by the brilliant branding of Tiffany's. You do overpay for jewelry. But it comes in that Blue Box that we have come to believe represents the pinnacle of quality. But more. It says, if you buy there, then you are special, and so is the person you give the gift to. Packaging and branding is the name of this game; the markups are huge, sometimes in the hundreds of percentages.

Most of the real lessons in life we learn from the mistakes we make, the tough stuff, not the triumphs. A friend of mine, my will and estate lawyer, is quite a good writer. He has compiled a list, a book idea

he calls "100 Dumb Mistakes Even You Can Avoid." My own addition to this list would be, "Other than your engagement ring, or a
strand of good pearls, *never* buy jewelry thinking it will appreciate
in value."

For years, I bought jewelry for my wife, almost always estate pieces
from high-end stores on Newbury Street in Boston, Madison Avenue
in New York, or from special people in the trades, such as pearl people,
or diamond people, all in somewhat seedy offices that spoke to me of
"bargain prices" and "only for the few" deals.

Jewelry was always bought for special occasions: big birthdays or
major anniversaries. My father was frugal, some would say cheap. But
he believed for years that gold, for a long while $40 or $50 an ounce,
would appreciate greatly. The year I was married, gold was around
$35 an ounce. This was because he also believed that all governments
would eventually devalue their currencies and that gold would soar
during these inflationary periods. So he bought gold jewelry for my
mother, gold cuff links for himself. He said, "Forget creativity in jewels. Only a connoisseur can figure what design means in price. But if
you melt gold down, you get the current price of gold according to
weight. Everything else is mostly crap and not worth much." I have
several pairs of Dad's cuff links, 18-karat gold. Each of the links is
about an ounce. He paid hundreds of dollars. Now gold is worth about
$1,200 an ounce. Pretty good investment. But not for him. He died
in 1974, when gold was about $180 an ounce. Sometimes if you think
you see the future, you're going to be too early to profit from it. My
measure of this is that Van Gogh knew he was a genius, but practically
the only person who bought his paintings was his brother, and the artist
died a failure in the eyes of the world, which measures everything by
your net worth.

Sometime after Susan died, I brought a lot of her jewelry into someone I trusted, the owner of a business established in my city for many
years. I wanted appraisals, wanting to sell the ornate, clunky pieces.
All lovely, I thought, but the younger generations are never going to
go to waltz evenings, formal balls, or dress-up weddings where jewels
and medals will be worn. They will mostly wear gimp bracelets, or
ones made of knotted rope or bearing mottos on rubber celebrating a
charity 10K. Not ruby and diamond necklaces or pins. They're all just
stuff and can be rented if you're invited to a coronation.

The appraisals came in at less than *half* of what I had paid for the items. "I like to think that I'm not naïve." I said to the dealer, "Most of these pieces I got from wholesalers, special people to whom I had to be *referred* to even get in to see them."

The dealer laughed. "Everyone thinks they're sophisticated," he said. "They come in and say to me, 'I have this guy in New York, very hush-hush, deals in emeralds.' I suppose you have a guy, too."

"I had a bunch of guys," I said. "For diamonds. And pearls. And furs."

"Well," he said, "this is a business of secrecy, sleight of hand. The markups can be obscene, and there's no way of changing it. So you can go to a reputable dealer who's been in business a long time, and then they screw you a little less than 'the guy in New York.' Or they could screw you more. Or you could go to an auction house and take your chances. But the houses take a big bite out of the proceeds."

My estate lawyer told me that one of *his* clients, a jeweler, would buy silver necklaces for 30 cents in Thailand and sell them to his customers for $30.

Here's my own scenario to you on the jewelry game, in simple terms.

You buy an antique estate piece, lovely design, with small diamonds, rubies. For instance, you pay $1,000 for it. When you, or your beneficiaries, sell it, the dealers pay you $400 or $500. Then they resell it to a new buyer for $1,000 or $1,200. Then that buyer or *his* beneficiaries sell it back again for $400 or $500. And the dance goes on.

The dealer also told me, "One of our competitors had lunch with me a few years ago. And *he* told me that every customer he deals with he tells, 'Buy this ring. In time it will be a *great* investment.'" He laughed. But I didn't laugh at my own stupidity.

Losing money on any investment opportunities offers lessons. And my jewelry adventures proved to me that in this arena, it's no different from how the minute you drive your new vehicle off the car lot, it's already depreciating. And I don't need to hear exceptions to the rule. Most of you reading this will never be experts in jewelry, or antique automobiles.

If you take pleasure in a ring, pin, or necklace, take pleasure in wearing it. I treasure small family pieces, cuff links particularly. Cherish these and pass them on. But do not think they are going to bring you a bonanza when you sell them. I now get somewhat angry when I see all the holiday ads for jewelry. "Don't do it!" I say out loud to the advertisements. None of us likes to feel like a sucker, but it's a good lesson if we don't repeat the same mistakes.

**Unless you're an expert, never treat jewelry purchases
as a great investment.**

CHAPTER 43

SOCIAL OR COUNTRY CLUBS

All of you have social lives, both virtual and real. We are still an aspirational society. Most of us want to do well, to climb up various ladders, both in business and with our peers, that group, or groups, of friends who also aspire to certain things. These are benchmarks of adult life.

My two partners and I have 2,000 clients all over the world. Many are hardly what you would call rich. But they all teach me interesting things that enrich me every day, far more than in a monetary sense. They have been and are plumbers and carpenters, artists and musicians, union members and chief executive officers, heads of foundations, writers, teachers, venture capitalists, old and young, gay and straight, and men and women.

All of them belong to various associations or clubs. Some of those clubs are not open to the general public. And Americans have always been keen on being in with the in crowd, wherever that in crowd resides, regardless of party or religious affiliation. Life is unfair, of course. But sometimes it's unfair in your favor. Most of us want to belong to something, whether it's Veterans of Foreign Wars, the Kiwanis, or a golf course where you have to get letters of recommendation from members.

I know people who have desperately wanted to join certain clubs in various cities and have been refused membership, or told not to apply. Others have been outright blackballed. The term comes from the English, the originators of private, upper-class clubs. You'd be proposed for membership and a meeting would be held. Instead of a show of hands voting in or out, members would pass a box around the long dinner table. The box would have a hole in the top. The members would have small, marble-like balls: one white, one black. As the box was passed, each member would drop a ball into the hole, white or black. One black ball could keep you out. Cruel, of course. I know people who, when blackballed, sold their house and left the community. None of us would enjoy driving by the gates of a place that would exclude us, places that found us not worthy of membership.

The comedian Groucho Marx commented, "I don't want to belong to any club that would have me as a member." But there now is a Groucho Club in London, for journalists. And you could be excluded from that if the members didn't like the cut of your jib. There is an old line about becoming a member of a club: "Pull up the gangplank; I'm aboard." This means, "I'm in and I don't care if anyone else ever is allowed." Human nature.

So for all of you who don't even know that this might be important to your social or business life, remember this: if you have a chance to join something in a new city or town because a new friend or business associate will sponsor you, say . . . yes. Because if you live someplace for a long time, you can build up enemies as well as friends. Or people who resent you, for all kinds of reasons, and would be happy to keep you out.

You think this is a cynical take on membership in anything? I want you to understand how the world works and thinks.

Join clubs early in life, before a list grows of people who would exclude you.

CHAPTER 44

THE INCREMENTAL PAIN IN THE BUTT THEORY

My first boss told me, "If you have a problem that can be solved by throwing a little money at it, it's not a problem." He called it his "incremental pain in the butt theory."

Often in this social networking environment, time seems to be one of our biggest challenges. *No time* is more like it. And little downtime for ourselves without endless interruptions, including our own obsessive checking for messages and information on smartphones and tablets.

Here's an example of simplifying a pain in the butt with holiday shopping frustrations. I have to Christmas or holiday shop for several dozen people: family, office staff, and various folks who have helped me in wonderful ways during the year. The process could take me days to complete, partly because I like to go into stores, see and touch the merchandise, and talk with the people who sell and buy the products. It's also partly how I do research about spending habits and what the buying public is thinking about. It helps me strategize and manage people's money to be in the thick of life, not merely online. Shopping that way can make things easy, but teaches me nothing.

So it could take me a few hours over several days to hit a variety of stores in different locations, often paying multiple parking lot or garage fees, getting caught in traffic, and waiting in lines. Expensive and not a jolly experience. For years I've taken a few hours off from work, usually on a Tuesday or Wednesday, starting at 1:30 after lunchtime when stores, even in holiday season, are much less crowded. Then I hire a car service to take me to multiple locations, waiting for me to emerge and plug the packages into the trunk. In 3 hours, I've done all my holiday shopping and never had to think about the pain in the butt of logistics.

Another example is making sure you cement relationships with people who take care of you during the year: contractor, plumber, electrician, snowplow people, yes, everyone; many people pay little attention to them. But they are crucial to making your lives easier. Cash is an easy gift at the holidays. But cash doesn't linger in the mind long enough. Everyone *does* remember a HoneyBaked ham, though, which I send to all the key people who make my life easier during the year. And the hams become anticipated and relished and help you establish a certain branding: *The HoneyBaked Ham Man* is a nice way to be remembered. The thought and act bind them to you. And HoneyBaked Ham does all the work.

It's smart to brand your personal life almost as much as your business and career.

Occasionally, what seems like an extravagance can turn something complicated into a pleasure.

CHAPTER 45

EVERY FAMILY IS A SOAP OPERA

You're not the only one who thinks that your family is dysfunctional or crazy. Only families in denial think they put a perfect face out to the world. I love the people who send out tales of their family adventures during the holiday season. I kept a classic example of this in a bookshelf in my office; the beautiful family's picture is displayed for all to see.

"Your family?" newcomers ask.

"Nope," I answer, "just a shining example." The attractive parents have four children: two boys, two girls. The letter inside of the card talks of prizes, trips, and jobs at *Vogue*, Goldman Sachs, and Disney. And that's just the kids. The parents love each other desperately, dominate the nonprofit boards of their city, and go to Davos, Mustique, and the Aspen Institute. This letter was so over-the-top that if you took it at face value, it was enough to ruin your holidays. The truth is often the opposite of the perfect family, and those holiday letters make almost all of us, the recipients, share the same gag reflex because we know that most of the holiday reports are wishful thinking, putting on the bold face.

Many of you reading this have come from divorced parents. You've sadly built up scar tissue from dealing with this while growing up. It hurts. My parents stayed married until my father died. But they fought constantly and armed silence often ruled the household. They stayed with it partly because that was the norm. I had met only two people who came from divorced parents until I got to college. And those two people were brothers, older than I, who were terrific athletes, and no one felt sorry for them, because they were jocks. Children are more resilient than parents. They get smart enough at early ages to play the guilt of Mom and Dad like drums, knowing that often *both* parents will spoil them. But divorce hurts. Two of my closest male friends in the world, one brother-in-law and one college roommate, both broke down in tears to me on separate occasions about the divorce of their parents. Both of these admissions came just after college graduation, fueled by alcohol and a time when one chapter closed, with new chapters ahead, and facing a life after school, it was time for some honesty. Do you feel better knowing that there are families much more dysfunctional than yours? Not really. You cannot make up the true things in life mostly in the horrible or despicable department. But this partially is why we all search for love and understanding as we get out into life. We hope that love can erase the scars from the past. I think it does help to believe that love is out there. I know that once that belief ceases bad things scurry in and hope erodes.

One of my closest friends, a woman, grew up in a very unhappy household, with a tyrannical father and a mother who allowed herself to be tyrannized, belittled, and demeaned. She has one sibling, a brother. My friend is funny, optimistic, and determined to win in whatever she pursues. Her brother has had nothing but mistakes, bad fortune, and a mostly unhappy life. "He's lost in the past," my friend said. "He cannot get over the traumas of childhood. He replays the movie constantly, instead of focusing on the *next* movie, which may be a comedy. I now laugh at childhood and focus on the other side of the mountain *ahead*. If the Pilgrims only obsessed about leaving Holland where would we be?"

Good thoughts for all of us who fear being dragged down into the swamps of family.

Keep looking for the new chapters, not the rereading of the old ones.

CHAPTER 46

FATHERS AND SONS

One of the toughest times in life is when (and it will happen) the son or daughter becomes the father or mother to a parent who is still alive. There is no real preparation for this. Partly because none of us really expects death. Often it is sudden, without warning. In a Freudian sense, the son *has* to exceed the father, to do better, get richer, and become more successful. This is cosmic, in the bone, and I believe it. There are many problems with fathers and sons beyond Freud, no matter how much love exists between them. It's sometimes a tender but, more often, a fractious journey.

I had a tough father who never went to college. He was orphaned at 11 and, instead of spoiling me, he wanted to make sure that I never had an entitled bone in my body, and that if I ever had any creature comforts in life, I would have to earn them myself. "Just assume," he drummed into me, sometimes with a belt, "that no one else is ever going to give you anything. If they do, it's an accident."

In all of this it will help if you have a sense of humor, particularly an appreciation of the absurd. This is for your own self-protection because dwelling on the past too much can bring you down.

Guilt is a dangerous emotion and the one that probably causes more distress within families than any other.

When my father died suddenly, I was 37 years old. We worked together, something I would not advise for my readers. When people say, "Boy, how wonderful you could work with your dad," this is like people saying to you, "You look just great." You probably *don't* look great, and it is almost never "wonderful" to work within a small family business. For a long time when I was a rookie stockbroker, I was completely under my tough dad's thumb. This actually was the trigger for me to become a writer, to free myself from business and my father's authority. "When my first book is published," I thought, "I'm outta here." But when that happened several years into my apprenticeship, I had made the amazing discovery that stock markets' movements were largely emotional. Not about math, but fear and greed. Emotion and character study, I know, were the only things I really understood. So I stayed in the business and wrote on the side.

As time went on in the office, and I emerged from under the thumb, a strange change occurred. As my father got older, he depended more on me. The son, bit by bit, was becoming the father. This was as bad as or worse than being the rookie, in my view. There is no freedom in a family business. You're locked into the past with layers of angst you have to confront every day. I'll get pushback on this subject. But I've dealt with endless clients and friends over the years, approaching this subject. It's created many more complications in lives than it has happiness. When my dad died we were about to knock heads about many issues. Here's another observation you might ponder: no matter how much love exists between fathers and sons, the saddest day of your life, when he passes on, is also the most liberating day. No guilt here: it's the normal turning of the wheel.

In many cases the experience motivates the sons and drives them to exceed the father. Dick Smith springs to mind, the former chief executive officer of General Cinema and Neiman Marcus. Smith's father ran a string of drive-in theaters in the Boston area. I remember my dad saying, "The kid will never come up to the father." But young Smith drove forward, achieving success his father could have never dreamed of. Ned Johnson at Fidelity is another standout example. His father was a legend in the financial world, but his son took Fidelity to levels his dad probably could never have predicted. But most sons for their sanity should be tossed out of the family business boat to make their own way in life and show the world what a strong son can accomplish, and I don't think fathers are necessarily doing their kids a favor by naming them Junior much less "the third."

You know the old country song, "Mammas Don't Let Your Babies Grow up to Be Cowboys"? Don't put them in the family business, either. Too many broken relationships, acrimony, and lawsuits can come out of it.

Save your sanity, your manhood, and don't go into the family business.

CHAPTER 47

WHEN FAMILY OR FRIENDS ARE AFFLICTED

All of you have had or will have family and friends afflicted with very bad health and personal issues. Sometimes illness strikes and lasts for a long time. It lingers and wears down not only the one who is ill but also numbers of people, close by blood or friendship. A long, sad journey. The bad news can also arrive with a sudden bang: a stroke, a heart attack, an accident, a suicide, or a murder. I have known all of these.

Most of us, in these situations, ache for our friends but hesitate to call because we don't want to intrude or bother anyone. Then guilt sets in. "Should I call? Or not call?" I learned a lot while my wife was undergoing treatment for lung cancer, including what to do when friends are going through difficult times. I learned that even though well-meaning people called at tough or inconvenient times, the calls meant so much to me and to my children. I will never forget the kindness of the callers.

People honestly don't know what the right thing to do may be. When Susan was first diagnosed, we received enough flowers and plants to open a small shop. "I'm not dead yet" was her reaction. Again, people mean well, but they feel helpless and try to do their best.

There are several ways to deal with this situation as a friend or as a *really* good acquaintance or coworker.

In the friend category, suck it up and make the phone call. It does take a gulp and an effort. But you'll be happy you did it.

If you're not quite a good friend, or if you work with the person who has been injured, or is in treatment or rehab, get his or her address and write a *real* note, not an e-mail or text. Something innate in all of us, I think, likes to feel the heft of something we can hold, feel, and open up, such as an envelope.

We tend to take something we can feel is tangible more seriously.

And it means so much to the person who is on the other end of these notes.

I would say no to flowers. Flowers seem too final to me, too easy, in a way. I would remember more the hard stuff. Tough to make a phone call, but very meaningful.

As for sending a book, lovely, but seldom read, and may demonstrate that you don't really know the person very well, or his or her tastes.

Never be afraid to phone someone who means something to you, if he or she is in need. The person will always remember that you called.

CHAPTER 48

GO TO THE SOURCE

Never underestimate the value of face-to-face contact. Here's a short story that perfectly illustrates this theme.

You know by experience that dealing with bureaucracies of all kinds can drive you nuts. Particularly when it comes to government at all levels. The petty tyrants we have to bow to, to realize their power. I've had various audits by the Internal Revenue Service (IRS), including by agents who couldn't really speak English. And the fake respect for the taxpayer is so transparent as to be ludicrous. One auditor questioned a check I had written for the Stanford Court, a hotel in San Francisco, where I had stayed on a business trip that I claimed as a tax deduction. She disallowed the expense because "Traffic tickets are not a deductible expense." She thought the word *court* meant a court of law. I've learned that for audits, it's best not to represent yourself. Let your accountant do it. It takes emotion out of the equation. It will not help you if you lose it in front of the IRS.

In my apartment building there are several residents with disabilities. We really are not a politically connected building, and the city removed a handicap space we'd had for some time. I called several politicians to see about getting it restored, with absolutely no results. I was bounced around to a number of other people, and the bureaucratic game went on with no success. I've never had much juice on the political front. Mostly because, unlike most of my friends, I've never much been in love with politics or politicians.

But there is no force on Earth more powerful than a determined woman. One of my neighbors has a child with a physical disability, and she became fed up with the process. She went to City Hall, found the right department, and camped in front of the office of the person in charge, also a woman. Because my neighbor was persistent, also charming and smart, she won over the woman in charge. So much so, they emerged friends from the meeting. Literally 3 hours later, a truck from the city arrived. The crew dug holes and planted two signs heralding our new handicap parking space, right outside our front door.

Having a legitimate complaint ensures nothing in life. But if you show up for face-to-face meetings, and are charming, with a touch of a sense of humor, you can perform certain small miracles. And if you are passionate but reasoned. Never strident. This can never happen as effectively as when you use the human touch.

**If you want to solve problems, show up in person.
Being face-to-face often makes these
problems go away.**

CHAPTER 49

PHILANTHROPY

The rhythms of life should include thoughts of charity or philanthropy. This usually begins early in one's forties. That's when you have marriage, family, and career somewhat put into place and you start to look around. You look at what else might be important to a life that has meaning, including what we leave behind.

As all of you get older, you will be increasingly assaulted by daily mailings from all kinds of institutions asking for your money. Almost all of these causes are worthy and deserve support. But it's impossible to take care of everybody and everything.

This is how the *giving* part of your life usually takes shape. Some friend of yours will call you and say, "I'm doing a bike ride for breast cancer. My sister died of this and I'd love your support for this incredible cause." And you're happy to send your friend a check. Or a friend or business associate will call and say, "I just joined the board of our favorite museum. You love art. How about talking to a few of our people to explain how great this place is? They're looking for someone like you to join as well." This happened to me when a client called me about the board of the Boys and Girls Clubs of Boston: "We are the best server of disadvantaged youth in the city, thousands of kids at our clubhouses." First of all, when clients ask for something, it's likely that you'll respond positively. You scratch my back; I'll scratch yours. This is how the game is played.

Once the philanthropy itch presents itself, it triggers memories of its own. My grandfather, as an immigrant to Boston, chose the settlement house the West End House as his favorite nonprofit. Because it was a place that nurtured him when he was young and a refuge where he could play baseball, run, learn to box, and have mentors to put him on the road to being truly American. He never forgot it and eventually he donated the money to build a recreation hall at the summer camp the West End House eventually built in New Hampshire.

Joining Boys and Girls Clubs' board has enriched me in so many ways as I watch many young people who will never forget the roads the experience the Clubs put them on. And I can honor the memory of my grandpa as well.

Early in your philanthropy experience you will gravitate toward institutions, such as the Boys and Girls Clubs or your college. It will be friends or clients or customers who get you involved. Eventually your philanthropy will include hospitals that serve your family, or your giving will be disease oriented, such as research of cancer or diabetes treatments, after loss has sadly entered your lives.

The counting on you for your money will be relentless; the busier you are in life, the more the asking will increase and almost every cause is worthy. Here are my suggestions for handling the deluge of envelopes seeking your money. Be disciplined. Know your three or four most cherished causes and concentrate on those. "Sorry," you can say, "I know you're passionate about what you believe in, but I have a list of causes dear to me and my family, and I want to concentrate on my giving to *them*." Be firm and up-front and everyone calling you will understand. Stick to your guns and this process will be less stressful or aggravating.

Occasionally when people have complained to me about the level of giving I do, I have told them, "Look, I have a trust which is drawn up for various givings. My trustee is brutal and he is in total control of those funds. 'Dr. No' I call him, and often I cannot get him to budge. So sorry . . ." This deflects people's expectations. Fall back on the mythical trustee.

One other bit of advice on the subject of other people's money: folks may think you're half-baked rich. But my dad cautioned me, "Never count anyone else's money. You'll be wrong in *both* directions." Dad was right.

If you *do* get to the point in your lives when you can make substantial pledges to your favorite causes, *bleed* the funds out to the institutions. Stretch the giving over a period. Fund-raising is both a noble and a cynical profession. Believe me; most organizations love you for the money, not for your charm. If you pay a pledge off immediately, they're on to whoever is next on the list—and the work of development, fund-raising, never stops. They do not rest on laurels. If you parcel out your giving, they'll continue to invite you everywhere and the courtship goes on. Once you're tapped out on your gift, it's almost like a romance that's over and you've been dumped. Occasionally it's good to be a little cynical as well as generous.

Don't count other people's money. You'll be wrong in both directions.

CHAPTER 50

KEEP THE MARKERS OUT THERE

A *marker* is slang for what one owes a bookie or loan shark. Someone to whom you owe money, usually at very high interest rates. You agreed to pay because you were a gambler or really needed the money that no one else would lend you. The marker was a note that you signed. The word is also called a *chit,* as in, "I've called in the chit."

I once had a friend who was Sicilian and grew up in California. Her family, most of whom lived on Long Island, New York, were rumored to be connected to certain relatives who could supply you almost anything, because "it fell off the truck." She was the first person I ever knew who used the expression "He's dead to me." Long before *The Sopranos* marched onto the stage. Years ago, she and her best buddies had a favorite restaurant in the Back Bay section of Boston. They were regulars. But one night, the maître d' was *so* rude to them, so dismissive and insulting, that they fled in dismay and anger. When she told me the story, I said, "Why don't you make the call?" meaning, jokingly, that she call her relatives on Long Island.

She took it seriously. "I'd never do that," she said.

"How come?"

"Because then I'd owe them. And you don't want to owe them."

I treat this subject, favors for others, as if it's a kind of savings account, something to use in a rainy-day situation. I like to help other people. Maybe it's insecurity, I'll admit. But there's satisfaction in solving problems that people don't seem able to solve themselves.

This is not a suggestion to lend or give people *money* to help them out. If money is involved, most often the recipient resents the giver and seeks to distance himself or herself from you.

Sooner or later, though, you're going to be needy yourself, and you're going to have to reach out to the network you've helped in the past. Someone I advised repeatedly, years ago, at various crossroads in his life, on how to open certain doors in our city to his long-term benefit, eventually rose and prospered, partly from these sessions. When one of my children needed advice *and* a job at a critical time, I called in a marker. I never like to do this. But you *will* do things for your children and grandchildren you'd never do for anyone else. Sometimes it's for the wrong reasons. But "blood is blood," as my Sicilian friend also pointed out.

So, build up the markers, like miles benefits on credit cards. But have long memories for when you have to call them in.

Do more for others than they do for you. But take note of those favors.

CHAPTER 51

RAISING CHILDREN

This will be a short chapter but a very important one. Many of you reading this already have children, or eventually, will have them. If you don't, chances are you have nephews, nieces, or godchildren and can observe, from a loving distance, how they're being raised. Mostly, when viewing others' children we tend to be critical. With one's own kids, at a certain age, when they're out of the parents' home, we can see and understand everything. But, once they're out, we cannot do a damn thing about it.

I was a counselor at several camps in Maine from late high school till early college days. It was a great summer job and freewheeling in the days when parents did not hover. They actually believed the camps would do a great job with their children for *eight* weeks. And everyone would get a vacation from one other. Virtually everyone I knew growing up had this experience, and loved it.

Well, times change. So do revolutions: analog to digital, the characters, and the fads. But human nature is immutable; it never changes.

I have three children, two boys and a girl, and five grandchildren. I think the best single piece of advice I could give you on child rearing is to *be consistent*.

What do I mean by this? Partly to say that you cannot always be best buddies to your kids. There are times when you have to be a parent, an adult, with a pecking order in the house that starts with the grown-ups and descends to the kids.

Aside from consistency, always try to make sure that your children can never complain that any one child was the favorite. All my three children's lives, they have pounded my wife and me with the phrase

"Am I number one?" They'd say it to tease. And we'd always respond, "Nope, you're number three." The truth is that someone always was number one or number three, depending on what day it was, the ebb and flow of family life. But we never betrayed the truth. So no matter what the punishment or praise that we parceled out, the kids could honestly feel they were treated equally. And loved equally. My dad occasionally would say to me, "I always love you, but sometimes I don't like you very much." The truth does hurt. And one thing you do not want to happen to children is having them lost in the past. It is almost always destructive.

One last thing: we all hear the "click" in life at different times, the period when we finally get it. It can take years for the click to happen for your children. And yes, for some, that day never comes. But you can never give up on a child of yours; you often have to play through the pain.

Many high school yearbooks have a section that pick "best athlete," "most beautiful," "brainiest," and always, "most likely to succeed." Looking back at this last item, in my experience with many "most likely to succeeds," their finest hour was senior year in high school. They peaked then and most never achieved the success their classmates predicted.

Another eternal truth may give you comfort as parents. It comes from one of my favorite lawyers, a woman, street-smart, with endless experience with families. After practicing law for many years, including divorce work, she was a Superior Court judge, practical and profane. "When it comes to raising children," she told me, "just remember . . . all teenage boys are assholes."

I wouldn't argue with a judge.

**Above all, be consistent in the treatment
of your children.**

CHAPTER 52

MARRIAGE

I was married for 45 years and have written about or observed hundreds of other marriages, maybe many more than that. My team and I watch over several thousand people's financial lives, and you can tell by now that it's a very psychiatric business the way we run it. In Susan's and my marriage, we had an early rule: in any controversy, whoever had the stronger opinion, who cared most, won. Two times my wife wanted us to move: once from the suburbs to the city, once from a house in the city to an apartment. I was not so sure, but not adamant, about the subject. My point of view was the pain-in-the-neck part of moving, not so much the concept.

"I'm going to do 90 percent of the organization anyway," she said.

She was right. We moved both times. In each case it proved wonderful.

I wanted our second son to go to the summer camp in Maine where I had been a counselor. Susan resisted. Her summer camp experience had been marginal at best. In fact, she'd hated every minute of camp. I won that potential battle because I cared about it much more than she did. Now my youngest grandson goes to the same camp. Lots of beats go on and on in life, if you're lucky. Marriage involves compromise more than anything else, and strategy, if you're smart, assuming you both *want* to keep it all together. One of my clients for a long time was one of the creators of the children's series *Curious George*. Her name was Margret Rey, a very difficult person who suffered fools not at all and considered most people at *first* blush to *be* fools, until they proved otherwise to her very exacting tastes.

When she was first referred to me, she came into my office, which was on the twenty-fifth floor of a Boston building overlooking the harbor.

"Take a look at this view," I said to Margret.

"Forget about that," she said in her strong German accent. (She and her husband had bicycled across France to Spain to escape the Nazis). "What are you going to do with my money?" Cut to the chase, or rather, cutting through the crap, was her hallmark.

A neighbor of hers told me, after Margret died, "I met Hans Rey on the street one day and I asked him how he managed to live in peace with his wife for many years. Hans Rey looked at me and smiled in a resigned way. 'In our marriage,' he said, 'we agreed that being together, *I* would make all of the big decisions, Margret would make all the small ones.' He hesitated, like a good actor. And then said, 'So far there have been *no* big decisions.'" They were married for 42 years.

In many ways, marriage is somewhat of an unnatural act. My dad, when he disapproved of someone I was dating after college, told me, "There are a thousand women at least, from here to California, that you could fall in love with and marry. It's just a matter of being *out* there for you to decide."

I think this is right. I was in love before I met Susan. It was an intense relationship, two people on the cusp of careers, trying to one-up each other intellectually. As if the romance were a contest, "too hot, not to cool down," as the great songwriter Cole Porter wrote. The all-consuming nature of this relationship really almost left no room for anything else, and I think we both felt that. It drove us to end it, probably smart at the time, thinking with our brains rather than other parts. Unusual, as I look back, for people in their early twenties to understand self-preservation.

One big thing you should know as you enter marriage: people grow at different rates. Which can mean growing apart. We change and grow, or we don't change, and feel creeping doubts about the directions our lives are taking. If you don't think children can change everything in your lives, you don't live on this planet. My best test for getting married with your brain *first,* is this. Ask, "Will I look back on that person, years later, if I *didn't* do it and say, 'I *should* have married them'?" But you have to ask this question of yourself honestly.

"Will I regret it if I let her/him go?" If you say, "Yes, I will," to the question, then *do* it. Get married.

I must add that, of course, there is much more to say about the relatively new reality of gay marriage. But everything I've written here about what may seem to be about so-called traditional marriage, a man and a woman, is totally applicable to gay marriage as well. Vows are vows and very different people say them. But the problems of marriage transcend gender, and they will roll on forever.

A last word on marriage comes from one of my favorite rants these days about relationships in twenty-first-century America. "It's tough to define relationships these days," I rant, saying, "I'm in love with a goat, and the goat makes me very happy. I'll bet I can find someone to marry me to the goat." I told this to a woman I met not long ago. She had come to Boston from someplace mystical in the Southwest. She was highly spiritual in a Red Rocks of Sedona way, feeling the forces. She looked at me, staring intently. "That would be me," she said.

Anything's possible in modern America. Just be sure if marriage is on your mind that you and your intended have a strong sense of the ridiculous.

If you are going to get married, make sure you consult your brain as well as the other parts.

CHAPTER 53

DIVORCE

One of the smartest lawyers I've ever known told me, "Divorce often comes down to the pink plastic vase in the bathroom." This, of course, means that often in this process, pettiness rules. I laughed at this then. But now I know it's true, having been through hundreds of divorces of friends, clients, and family. I have seven first cousins and my only sister: *all* of them have been divorced. There's no guarantee of anything in life, but this seems like a singular family achievement. Part of it, I think, is an old family attitude of ours that implied, "No one is *ever* going to be good enough for you." Probably not a great concept to stick in the minds of your children. I had a best friend who told me, "My sister married a man who made TV commercials. They did not have a great relationship. And my sister talks to our mother 14 times a day. My wife is a hot ticket. She tells me, 'Your mother and your sister treat Robert like a temp, like someone who's been sent over by Manpower.'"

(The marriage didn't last.)

I live in a state that basically gives you a 50–50 split of assets in any divorce. An interesting statistic, considering that as many as 50 percent of all marriages still end in divorce. If you're on this sad path yourselves, here are a few things to consider: thoughts from several first-class divorce lawyers, two men, one woman. This chapter is really about containing your costs in this pitiful procedure.

First of all, after your almost-two-year slog through the muck, you'll probably end up exactly where you would have been financially if you had settled it in the first few weeks of the struggle. "It takes so long," Willy, the cynical lawyer, says, "it's basically a two-year charade, because the judges and the lawyers have this dance that stretches out there until, if the people involved didn't hate each other when it started, they will hate each other at the end."

Human nature sometimes wears down the cynical lawyer. But he's practical beyond anything else, and his worldview is typified by having seen it all. "Here's the biggest thing to remember in divorce: 'the limitation on your future happiness is your ability to be in the same room as your ex and have a cordial conversation.'" Bertrand Russell, the philosopher, said this.

Read this previous quote over again, and let it sink in. Poisons can creep into your system, the more experiences you have. And a divorce that was bad and never really resolved can haunt your future.

But Willy goes on, with his road map, getting you to your new single life. Willy tells me, "The divorce lawyers know instantly what the settlement will be. Remember: lawyers will always give you a great first meeting. Because lawyers are actors. And after the first meeting, the relationship is often colored by *in*attention to you, not attention, which will drive you crazy. There's an old joke about the three biggest lies: one of them is 'check in the mail.' I think the fourth biggest lie is 'and it's all amicable.' The process goes on for so long usually, that by the second year, after endless delays for hearings etc., emotions take over and anything that *was* cordial, falls apart."

My cynical lawyer is also a romantic. He's just seen too much madness. But his last line to me, in a marriage, I think is right on the money: "You have to eventually find a friendship."

My second divorce lawyer is less aggressive, a peacemaker. But he is on his fourth marriage, which means he has probably learned a lot. I like to think that he's an incurable optimist, refreshing in an age that seems lost in "what could've been."

He has his sardonic side but is always romantic. Now he even seems a bit wistful and philosophical, too. "I think the process takes so long because of a certain ambivalence between the parties. If they try to rush it there can be unnecessary fighting. Time," in his view, "helps get the parties to get more practical. A good divorce lawyer doesn't make things worse. It's like gestating a baby, divorce is, it works better when both parties are getting to like their independence. Take it slow and build a new and civil relationship apart. It's often *worse* when it's quick and easy. *Then* husband and wife get in tremendous fights, accusing the first lawyer of imbecility."

"So what's most important?" I asked him.

"Humor on the lawyer's part is good. Not gallows humor, but self-deprecation. My mentor in the law taught me, 'You were meant to *serve*, not to lead.'"

My last divorce lawyer takes no prisoners. Suzanne has a somewhat jaundiced view of human nature. But she has seen a lot as a lawyer and then as a longtime judge. The judge is funny, too. "Down and dirty" I call it, no-nonsense, giving off the vibration, "I know more about human nature than you; listen to me."

"First of all," the judge says, "as far as timing is concerned, in big states forget it, you're doomed. Our Superior Court is now assigned 800 or 900 cases *per judge* in the single-docket system. You *can't* rush it. So here's my advice for the divorcing couple, because there is nothing in the system for flexibility. Remember that in divorce it's *not* about the money. It's hatred. It's that feeling that *someone* is going to greener pastures. And the aggrieved party wants to grind the other into the ground to satisfy the bloodlust.

"Remember this if you are about to separate: it is much better to give the money to your kids than to the lawyers. People tend to often get divorced for stupid reasons. You're going to be parents for the rest of your lives, spend your money on college, not hatred."

Accept your faults; be cordial. Eventually it's for your own self-preservation.

CHAPTER 54

SOMEONE TO LOVE YOU

Life is a constant search for love. Sometimes, yes, in all the wrong places. Loneliness is a big deal in America today, with a high divorce rate, with countless dating and matchmaking sites trying to bring us together, out of the sadness of being alone. I used to think that the concept of arranged marriage was unthinkable. Now I think, "How could it be worse than the reality show that is modern marriage, presumably for love?" I have a godson who has had an arranged marriage. It appears to be wonderful so far. Some people say, "I love you" at the drop of a hat. Others almost never can say it, even if they feel it. My advice for all of you who see the full moon and feel the longing: know that this is one aspect of your lives where luck really plays a role almost more than anything else. I have friends who met their eventual spouse in high school. They never even dated anyone else. They've been married for many years. One of my best friends in college loves love. So much so that he's on wife number *four*. And he's said, "In sickness and in health," "for richer or for poorer," and "as long as we both shall live," *four* times. It's almost like the line "I'll be a little late tonight honey; start the fight without me." Love letters in the sand.

My wife and I worried a lot about one of our sons. He was single, living in New York City after some time in Los Angeles. He seemed to be throwing himself into work and had no one special in his life. I called him one day. "Your mother and I are worried that you're lonely."

"I may be alone," he said. "But I'm *never* lonely." It's a wonderful thing if you love what you do during the day. And his nightly adventures involved being the lead singer in a heavy metal band, often performing in the meatpacking district, way before it got somewhat fancy. He never went on before 1:30 AM and we never saw him perform.

"I don't have my meatpacking clothes," I told him when I couldn't watch his band.

"Not to worry, Dad," he said. "The crowd will think you're an agent from a record company."

Again the accidental nature of life. He met his wife-to-be, who was working in one of the clubs. She made baked stuffed lobsters on their first date, and they were off to the races.

When I read the wedding announcements in the Sunday papers, it seems that the vast majority of brides today are in their early thirties. This is probably 10 years or so older than in my generation's experience. Most of my male friends married whomever they were dating in spring of senior year in college. My two sisters-in-law were both 19 when they were married. My wife turned 22 on our honeymoon, and had all our three children by the time she was 26. It seemed as if we were all boys and girls then. Babies. We knew almost nothing about life, or about sex, either, for that matter. But there is no right or wrong way in marriage. Societies since marriage began have produced more jokes about that institution than anything else in joke history. With golf and religion way behind in the top 10 of the subjects lampooned.

Yes, fewer people are getting married. But living together in every combination you can name is livelier than ever. We need to belong to, and care for, someone. It's primal, and our partners need the same things back for themselves.

It's even tough to explain relationships today. I go on various rants quite often these days. Now I'm on a relationship rant. "You can't even define this word anymore," I hold forth endlessly. Leave it.

But everyone searching out there for someone feels exactly the way the medieval swains and maidens and the cave people felt. And everyone else through history felt. We all feel the same pangs and longings. "Who is going to love me the way I want to be loved?"

How do you do it? I have two secrets for finding love. One sounds obvious but perhaps not to everyone.

1. You have to force yourself to be out there: volunteer for causes you care about, walk for hunger, ride for diabetes . . . . Be part of the philanthropic world; join a Y or a university club. Take yoga classes, pottery lessons. It's difficult to go out there. It takes effort and you often don't feel like making an effort. You don't even feel like going out after work. But you have to.

2. You also have to force yourself to talk to strangers, when appropriate. At these lessons and lectures, at plays, at the gym, and at yoga. You can never tell where it might lead. In my view, the odds increase for mutual attraction if you meet by chance, not in virtual ways. My friends and family who have been involved in dating sites universally tell me how misleading the descriptions of the people they have met, for coffee, lunch, a drink, or dinner, are. We all are mostly looking for the same innocent thing. But life hasn't been innocent for a long time. When you've been burned or disappointed, or unlucky. (This is not a direct quote; observations).

Just in the last year or so, I have been intrigued with, or flirted with, women whom I've met at lectures, in restaurants, at the opera in Rome, at charity events, in stores, in elevators, and in parking garages. I tried to be polite always, low-key and friendly. But I'm trying to say things in introduction that may sound a little different to the person I'm attracted to. At intermission at the opera in Rome, I turned to the young woman next to me and said, "Look over the stage, still cut into the molding, 'Benito Mussolini.'"

"The glory of Rome," she answered. And we were off in our conversation.

She was Turkish and lived in Istanbul. She was a banker and loved opera, and traveled often to Italy to drink it all in. She had wanted to be a tennis pro . . . but her father had insisted she turn to business life. "There are strong traditions in my family," she said and shrugged. "But I pursue my passions elsewhere." She went back to Turkey and I to Boston. But we e-mail and her tales are priceless to me about the trends and politics swirling around her in the Byzantine Empire and the nightmare of the Middle East. This is not love, of course. But real dialogue can be a prelude to love.

I can remember summer jobs in high school and college, listening to love songs on the radio, seeing the big, yellow moons of July and August, and wondering whether real romance would ever come my way. "Do you believe in magic?" go to the lyrics of the old song John Sebastian wrote. I do believe, but I know that luck plays a role. But the more you're out there in life and not afraid to be original in approaching potential candidates, you can make your own luck. And find a love to go with a summer moon.

One cautionary bit of advice. In most cases, don't accept recommendations from family or friends in matters of the heart. They have preconceptions of you that have nothing to do with your understanding of what you want in a love interest. Their suggestions can be more annoying than helpful.

**Be open to *real* romantic adventures, not virtual ones.
Be *out* there.**

CHAPTER 55

MEDICAL SMARTS

Let's cut through the fog. Your internist, your primary care physician, will be one of the very few key people in your lives. Perhaps *the* key person.

Years ago, health–care benefits were way down the list of things employees cared about. Costs were reasonable, an afterthought. Job applicants almost never mentioned medical coverage as one of the top areas of discussion. It was a given as a benefit at most companies of any size. Salary, *money,* was the center of the issues. All the other concerns were way down the line.

Today, medical coverage seems to be the number one concern for people seeking work. I don't believe in retirement. I think that if we have life around us in a workplace, it keeps us involved. We don't feel certain aches and pains when we're concentrating on tasks at hand. And I believe, if the adrenaline is pumping because we have daily purpose in our lives, it helps produce a happier and healthier life.

Did I say that the most important thing you can do in your medical life is *make a friend of your doctor*? Because these days and forevermore, *you* are going to have to be your own best advocate in the health–care forest. If your doctor becomes your friend, and develops a stake in you, you have a chance to negotiate the frustrating slog through hospital nightmares.

My business team and I have 2,000 clients scattered all over the world. When any of them comes to our office for an appointment, we're animals about making sure that no one waits more than 5 minutes in the reception area. People can, and do, wait for hours for doctors to see them at appointments. It's almost as bad as the games the airlines play with all of us. And it's outrageous.

So, how do you separate yourself from the crowd to make sure that you and your family are cared for and not kept in waiting room hell?

Years ago, as a rookie in the business, with no network of friends, no clout, I learned early to do things a little differently, to force myself to find ways to get noticed.

For instance: I once developed a strange rash on one of my arms. It itched and was swollen, red, and hot to the touch. I got an appointment to see a dermatologist at one of the large teaching hospitals in our city. My appointment was at 2 PM. I checked in and was soon escorted to an examination room. "The doctor will be in shortly," I was told. After 40 minutes of waiting, I picked up a phone that sat on a small desk, called the operator, and asked her to transfer me to the nurses' station on my floor. When the nurse picked up, I said, "I've been waiting 40 minutes in this little cell. I've grown a second itchy head, which is why I came in here, and I'm about to run down the hall naked if someone doesn't see me within a minute and a half." A nurse arrived with a doctor in about 30 seconds. It worked. But why do we have to go through this frustrating exercise almost every time we have hospital experiences?

This week I took my primary care doctor, an incredibly smart and caring person, to dinner to grill him on the modern medical landscape and how to get some personal attention to efficiency and patient satisfaction. "Are we doomed in America now," I asked the man I called Dr. Stuart, "The Maven," "to accept being just a piece of anonymous meat when it comes to medical care? And are primary care physicians disappearing?"

"Well, it's a horrible way to make a living," he said. "But there will always be those who enter the field. Because they do it for the *people* not the money. I *did* and *do* it for the people I meet. And so do all the great internists I've known."

He continued. "I learn from my patients and they enrich my life. I don't engage with just wealthy patients. Some of my favorites have been a vice detective, and a man who carves elaborate duck decoys. I enjoy the clergy as well," Stuart said, "because we're in the same business. One Episcopal priest came to me, complaining that he was passing out when he was preaching and he couldn't cure it. 'I think it's my sins,' he told me. I figured out that it was his clerical collar. When he'd turn his neck in scanning the congregation, the collar would press on his carotid artery, causing him to lose consciousness. Problem solved, and it wasn't divine intervention. But the priest was like me. He was always available."

Dr. Stuart told me that there were several species of internists. "The first is my favorite," he said. "You stand the best chance of relating to this type. It's the 'Renaissance Man Doc.' They pursue things in depth and are excited by new ideas. I was an English major in college. I played the saxophone and took up the trumpet only recently. I love fly-fishing and I've kept bees. I take energy from my patients and I learn from them as well.

"But doctors get depressed," he added. "Because patients don't just get sick nine to five during the week. We need our hobbies. You'd be amazed how many doctors go to casinos to gamble.

"The second kind of internist is what I call 'The Machine,'" Dr. Stuart went on. "They love checklists, dot the *i*'s and cross the *t*'s. A lot of pediatricians are like this too. Test, tests, are what they call for. And I've seen a lot of these types giving you four shots of something a day. Check. Not thinking of any side effects that could be damaging. Machines are not very user-friendly.

"The next group of primary care docs couldn't qualify for surgery so they avoid any criticism from anyone by farming *everything* out to specialists. 'I think I hear a murmur,' they'll say. 'I'm happy to refer you out to check on it.' These are the safe haven doctors, cover everyone's tails.

"Lastly," said my maven doctor, "are the ones not interested in you for *you*. They're interested in the populations, only in you if you represent obesity, or diabetes, for example. These docs are basically bloodless. Their big picture is humanity as a headline. Don't say you weren't warned."

I asked him, "Why is it that doctors keep you waiting sometimes for over an hour from when your appointment was scheduled? I'm in a very personal, demanding profession also. If I keep a client waiting for more than 5 minutes, I feel embarrassed by it. And I have 2,000 clients. It drives people nuts."

"The biggest excuse given is that they need more time with the patients. That's probably a crock. The real reason is that doctors mostly are horrible at organizing their time. No one told them in medical school that they actually would be thrown out of the boat to run a business. One of the greatest doctors in history, Sir William Osler in England said, quoting Socrates, 'The art is long, and the work is hard.'"

So, how do you recruit a doctor like Stuart the maven to *your* side? Have a story, or, *stories,* to get him or her intrigued by you as an individual. And pay attention to your classmates, from grammar school, high school, and college. Search your city for your people from the past. They can connect you. Of course, social media is a key to this connecting. But be specific in asking for help in finding an internist or primary care doctor who falls into the Renaissance type, someone who will work both sides of the brain and is most likely to understand your needs. And who will respond in a smart, compassionate way. He or she should coax your fears from you as well.

So, you've turned out a few doctor names from your network. Google them or check Wikipedia for clues to their career progress and perhaps their hobbies. *Everyone has a hot button.* Years ago I tried without success to get an appointment with a podiatrist. I discovered that he was a fanatic about Winston Churchill and collected all sorts of items with the Churchill theme, including commemorative ashtrays. I called the office again and tried, "Tell him I know something about Winston Churchill that no one else knows." It worked and I got the appointment.

The first thing the doctor said to me was "Okay, I bit. What do you know about Churchill that I don't?"

I took a chance. "What you didn't know is that using his name got me an appointment."

He hesitated and then he started to laugh, came to me, and shook my hand. "You figured it out," he said. "Maybe I can learn something from *you.*"

I would bet that if you do your due diligence and make your approach to people personal, it could work for you, too.

These days you might write a short personal note, mentioning the doctor's interests or passions and then making comments about how a passion of yours could possibly appeal to him or her, make his or her life a little richer.

Is this technique honest? Well, once again in a country of 320 million people, do you want to stand in long lines? Or will you learn to be more creative in your approach to the care and attention we all hope to receive from others? Happy health care.

**Make your doctor your friend and find
his or her hot button.**

CHAPTER 56

TAKING CARE OF THE PEOPLE WHO TAKE CARE OF YOU

Most of the people I know deal daily with car valets, security personnel, support staff, landscapers, and contractors: plumbers, carpenters, electricians, tech support, all key to our lives in certain specific ways. But many of them are invisible to us. They move in and out of our lives and barely register in a personal sense. We pay our money to them, assuming they do their jobs with various degrees of satisfaction to us. And they remain anonymous to us. We seldom remember their names, and seldom care.

But if you pay a little attention in a personal way to those who take care of you, they can make your lives much easier, much more satisfying.

I live in the city and I park in garages every day, at my office and opposite my home. My first day at our office garage, I stopped as I entered and introduced myself to the attendant, asking his name and where he had grown up.

"Ethiopia," he said.

"Haile Selassie," I answered, "the Lion of Judah." Selassie had been the emperor of Ethiopia and a national hero. The attendant, Solomon, touched his heart and shook my hand, holding it in both of his, the Ethiopian custom. We became friends. Every day I came into the garage, he would put me in the first slot, the front of the line. Why?

Almost no other renter in the entire garage ever bothered to talk to Solomon about *his* life. He told tales of his family at home and the history of chiefs in his blood. He is a proud and worthy man; his stories painted pictures of Africa I had never heard, much more meaningful than words from a book.

In my summer community, I hired a contractor some years ago to build an addition on to our house there. Years later he built a small studio for me in back of our main house. I use it for writing and to run my money management business when I'm away from the downtown office. It's a small jewel of a structure, a colorful spot on the landscape like a cottage in the Adirondacks, a refuge for me and useful as a spillover for guests. I've told Al, my contractor, that he has the soul of an artist. "No one ever told me that," he said. And *that* is the point.

I invited him to a cocktail party and told him, "You can go anywhere in the world, have dinner with kings and queens, and if you wear a blue blazer and gray or black pants, you'll be dressed perfectly for almost *any* occasion. Get two blazers. One for winter and one for warmer months. And maybe two nice turtleneck sweaters: one wool, one cotton." He showed up in a blazer, smiling like he owned the place. And he got two new clients at the party.

"Thanks for being my friend," he told me when he was about to leave. It is often much more satisfying to get involved with individual people whom we can help get a leg up in life than to give checks to causes. Personal versus institutional can give rich satisfaction—and people can take pride, too, in knowing that the benefit is a mutual one. Al gives me incredible service in very creative ways. I introduce him to potential new clients for him. Mutually beneficial.

I need younger people in my life. In my money management business, to be successful, in my view, you have to be an information junkie. You have to stay current in relation not just to news that affects markets but also to trends: What are young people buying, listening to, collecting, watching, and reading? Being curious about all things helps you help clients more effectively.

I belong to a dining and social club in my city. It is a venerable place of distinction, the building a historical gem. It's also very old-fashioned in an age of decidedly lower standards at every level, including lack of civility. I dine there quite often and attend lectures, provocative and challenging for the mind. It reminds me of a past long gone.

Several years ago, the club employed a young waiter. He seemed to jump off the page at you, seeming to float in and out, from course to course, paying strong attention, somehow there but not there. I believe in asking questions of people. It's how we learn. "What do you really want to be doing?" I asked him.

He smiled. "I want to climb the ladder, to be a success in life," he said. I smiled as well.

The next time I came in for dinner, he handed me a copy of my latest book to sign for him. I was surprised and pleased as well. "How did you even know about this?" I asked.

"It's my business to be curious about people and things," he answered.

I helped him get a job with a leading financial firm, and his life is on a new path. He rewards me by telling me about the lives of his friends and what his generation thinks about the world today. And about *their* worlds too.

Mutually beneficial.

At the holiday season I remember these people who take care of me. I hope I add value to their lives and jobs as well. I send them all HoneyBaked hams, something everyone can use during the holidays. And something that may be a little different from what they get from others whose lives they help.

You can learn a lot from the people who take care of you. Pay attention, and they'll pay better attention back.

CHAPTER 57

LOSING A PARENT

Americans are increasingly forced to grow up faster than ever. A lot of the reason for this is the divorce rate, with the realities of tough stuff coming so early in life. Then you mix in the pressure of the technology revolutions swirling around us; not a lot of real childhood is available to the young, certainly little or no time for contemplation or playground pleasures.

My father grew up in New York City and was orphaned at 11. He was bounced from relative to relative, never going to college. He went directly to Wall Street, and just as he was starting to get somewhere, the Great Depression hit, and he was unemployed, feeling cursed. Losing his parents colored his entire life and set the pattern for his behavior, which was conservative and risk averse. Economic hard times made it worse.

But here is the lesson for you: he constantly gave me advice and counsel about what to expect in life, which he learned the hard way. Realism was his major message. Some of the lessons that he hammered into me were:

- "Remember, life is really hard, punctuated by moments of brilliance."
- "Life is work, whether you want to hear it or not."
- And a poem fragment by Thomas Gray: "All that beauty, all that wealth, ere gave, / Await alike the inevitable hour, / The paths of glory lead but to the grave!"

Heavy stuff.

Heavy, but, repeated often enough to take root in me. Lessons that have served me well, that taught me self-reliance and never to take myself too seriously.

My dad died in a hospital on his birthday, Christmas Eve, of a heart attack. I was 37 years old. It was a shock, no lingering illness, no deterioration, no long-term care. Bang! But he had prepared me for taking over the family. The best thing parents can do for their children is to give them advice honed from their long experience. And they should repeat the advice and repeat it, until it sinks in and sits in your brains, to be taken out as your own lives progress, like your grandmother's recipe for chocolate chip cookies.

My mother also was unsparing in her advice, and she loved having my friends around her house, reveling in their choosing *her* as their favorite mother role model because she paid attention to what *they* were interested in: their favorite movies, books, music, and courses of study. "She's like one of us," they'd say. "She understands. And forgives us our foolishness too." She, at times, when I'd be coming home late during college breaks, would be waiting up for me. "You're a drunken sot," she'd say to me. Or at other times, "Don't be a goddamn fool." She painted still lifes, played the piano, and read the *New York Times,* doing the crossword puzzle. She lived in Boston, but I always thought she longed to live in New York, to be a writer and run a salon where young and old would gather to laugh and think great thoughts. So, I think, I was prepared to live without my parents better than most, because of my parents' underscoring themes they believed in, and were not shy in drumming them into me. Very often, I know, I still think of her saying, when I'm about to go off various reservations, either in speech or action, "Don't be a goddamn fool."

So recalling lessons from a parent who is gone can make your new journey as an adult a lot gentler. Because you have a template of a parent's wisdom to ground you. And if you *disagree* with any of those lessons, it can help as well, because you're maturing enough to develop your own *lessons* of life. Bear all of this in mind, not to shy away from being an *adult* to your children, instead of just trying to be a buddy.

I think the best therapy you can give to surviving parents is, when visiting them, ask them about their childhoods and ask them where they went right or wrong. This will make visits less awkward, make you feel less guilty for all kinds of things. And make both of you feel much better. Your surviving parent will be helped, because we all love talking about ourselves, because we all love stories. You will learn a lot about yourself as well. This is advice for when you're alone with your surviving dad or mom. If other siblings are around, all bets are off, unless in that rare instance, your siblings all have the same points of view. Remember, *all* families can be killers in very different ways, if you let them. And if you know that you're the strong one in the family, and you feel that you're shouldering much of the load, the responsibilities for a parent, and you curse the fates that it seems to be *all* on you, just remember: it's a lot better to be the one with the broad shoulders than to be the *needy* ones.

As my mother told me, 'Try not to be a goddamn fool.'

CHAPTER 58

GETTING SMART LAWYERS ON YOUR SIDE

Unfortunately, you'll need a variety of lawyers in your life. But, you'll have to find *one* who can be the quarterback, your key legal person. He or she can direct you to the various other specialists in their fields who can help you and your family. An older lawyer, who was a client for years before he died, graduated from Harvard Law School in 1932 in the depths of the Great Depression. "If someone had offered me a job paying $10,000 a year for life," he told me, "I would have signed a contract in *blood*. That's how bad things were." He would tell me tales of hard times and good times. But he also stressed that there were always people who prospered in difficult business climates and that I would be well served by never following the crowd.

"Read George Orwell's novel *Animal Farm*," he told me. "In the beginning of the book, Orwell says, 'All pigs are equal, but some pigs are more equal than others.'" Remember these lines as you think about yourselves (which you do, all the time). How do you get to be one of those pigs that are more equal than others?

I learn a lot from the people who are Machiavellian, who don't think about the world in conventional ways. They think about getting the edge. They can help you to get the edge as well. My main lawyer handles my estate and trust issues. I describe him as quirky. But he may even be a shade darker than that. He wrote an unpublished novel years ago and sent it off to half a dozen publishers. They all sent it back to him with typical terse rejection letters. "None of the bastards even read it," he complained to me.

"How do you know that?"

He answered, "How do I know? Because between pages 39 and 40 in every manuscript, I put a hundred-dollar bill. They all came back to me. That's how I know."

That's the kind of person I want to have for a lawyer. He thinks of different ways to view the world on my behalf:

1. "Never go to a lawyer," he says, "unless you're introduced by a person who is in some way important to that lawyer. It may be his or her golf pro, or physical therapist, or investment advisor. Do not come in cold."

2. "Never go to a lawyer, though," he continues, "who handles anything for your *parents*. Because their first loyalty will be to your parents not *you*."

3. "You need a confidence level *before* you go into your first meeting. Be prepared in advance because most first meetings with new lawyers, they will be charming, conning you, if you will, at first blush."

4. "Know what *you* have going for you before you go in for your first meeting: Is it your brains? Is your family, but not your parents? Or is it your money? Or can you be the best finish carpenter, a specialty the lawyer can use, or someone who knows art or music or Flemish painters, to trade your expertise for that of the attorney?"

I spent an evening at dinner with several attorneys recently who each has at least 50 years of practice in different specialties, from labor law, to corporate, to utilities, to trial work. Two of them became judges, one of whom, the only woman, was on the Massachusetts Supreme Judicial Court, a person who brooked no nonsense.

"How would you pick a lawyer in *any* specialty?" I asked them. "How would you go about making them *want* to take care of you and your family in this increasingly anonymous society?"

Alan, my labor lawyer friend, is also cynical but full of humor and the sense that there is always a solution to legal problems if you're practical. "First of all," he said, "I will always see anyone who is recommended by a friend, or a person I *do not* want to disappoint. And *no* law firm *I've* ever heard of would not take your call and agree to meet with you. Lawyers, unlike doctors, do *not* have closed practices. They want the business."

Bob, a nonlawyer with us that night, said, "But you have to make yourself noticed, what with every professional you're seeking to hire, in any area where you're needy. For instance: in dealing with a serious medical condition I had a low point recently, being kept waiting in the doctor's reception area. I finally got to the end of a long line, and the nurse in charge said, 'How can I help you?'

"I looked at her and said, 'I could use a hug.' She jumped up and came around the desk and hugged me. 'You wait right here, honey. I'm going to make sure you're seen right away.'

"People respond to kindness in a cold world," he said to me, "whether it's in law, medicine, or other personal matters; you're needy, with a smile can do wonders. It's true."

And it is. Your impression on gatekeepers of all kinds can make a big difference for you.

Bob is a big user of lawyers in his business, his personal, and his philanthropic life. "The bigger the law firm, it seems," Bob said, "the bigger the bills. I got a bill for a letter my estate lawyer sent to someone for me. One page, $750. I told them that was outrageous.

"'It took a lot of thought,' the lawyer told me.

"I refused to pay it, and it was adjusted to $250. Still ridiculous. But the principle here is, if you don't pay attention to it, if the consumer doesn't set the value, you're going to be taken advantage of.

"It's like phone or cable bills. I called my phone provider and said, 'I can't pay your bills, I'm switching.' Immediately, no argument, they cut the bills by 40 percent. But they count cynically on people to never take the time to complain. Bitch and moan sometime. Out loud. It can help on almost everything you do. The squeaky wheel."

Bill, a former litigator and judge, held forth on today's law firms: "Well, these days you get twice as many lawyers coming out of school than can be employed as *lawyers*. So they have to do other things; the firms can't handle them. For a long time, the huge legal firms' mantra was, 'Grow or die.' And that theme has destroyed many big firms. Because lawyers cannot manage a business. They're not equipped for it. As a result of huge mergers, the costs became insane. Most mergers were like mixing ice cream and pickles. They don't work. And the desperation for revenue is so huge that they pile on work that is useless and expensive. It's all about the hours they bill. It results in dishonesty and needless overbilling."

His wife, Judy, an eminent jurist, tough-minded and fair, said, "Most law firms used to be small and efficient. It used to be a profession, not a bottom-line, inefficient machine. This need for revenue, so much work piled on, makes young lawyers hate it. And there's no institutional memory. Those lawyers got eased out. No time for mentoring. You want a lawyer for your personal needs? Think small. Try to never use the giants. Doctors increasingly don't put names on their patients. The huge law firms don't either. Make it small. And personal."

My friend Alan, always the cleanup hitter in the common sense department, said, "I had a meeting a few years ago with a large out-of-town firm interested in merging with us.

"'How much is your debt?' their senior partner asked me.

"'We have no debt,' I said.

"'Boy, an old-fashioned mom-and-pop organization, right?'

"'Yes, right,' I told him, 'if *mom-and-pop* means very *profitable and incredibly loyal to our clients.*' This firm I met with subsequently folded."

Whenever I seem to have a problem of almost any kind, I call Alan. He has the ability to cut through the fog and get to the point, even if the truth does hurt. I've known him since we were camp counselors in Maine together, both of us in college. He watched me shooting hoops one day then, on the outdoor basketball court.

"I have a feeling," he said, "that you probably peaked as an athlete in the eighth grade."

I need people on my team who can spot the character flaws when they walk in the door.

Pick your lawyers by their ability to cut through the fog and get to the point. There are professions where some cynicism is helpful.

Go small when you choose law firms; don't be an ATM for the big guys.

CHAPTER 59

LAST CHAPTER

People over 60 endlessly complain to me about the younger generations: they're entitled, they know nothing about history or the past, and they're lost in their smartphones, often while driving or walking in the middle of roads. Of course, it's easy to generalize about the generations, and none of you reading this wants to be lumped in with anyone. But I hear complaints about your cadre almost weekly, and please tell me if these stories fit in with your experience.

One client of mine, in Chicago, told me, "I have a great assistant. She's street-smart; she gets it, and she could have a terrific future. But many days, she comes in upbeat, incredibly happy. But after lunch, she has her head down, sour and unhappy. Where does this change come from? Well," he went on, "it turns out she's texting, all day. A boyfriend breaks a date, a girlfriend criticizes her, her sister has a problem. My assistant is great. But she's got no commitment, no sense of career path. You know what I'm talking about?"

I do. Because I hear stories like this all the time.

I wandered into an antique store outside of Boston this weekend and made an offer on a small French writing desk from the late 1800s. "How's business?" I asked the owner. I ask people in shops and restaurants and bars this question wherever I travel. It's how I like to do research, from the ground up.

"Pretty good," he said. "A huge uptick from a few years ago. So much so, that I'm telling you right now, I won't give you less than 10 percent off." We haggled a bit and I said, "About a month ago you had a young man helping you. He knew his stuff."

"Yeah," the owner said, "he did. But I let him go. All day he'd be on his whatever, smartphone. It was like he didn't have a job and the customers mostly were an annoyance to him. Work ethic? It's gone, like the Boston Braves, if you ask my opinion."

These brief stories can be like the Ghost of Christmas Past in Dickens's *A Christmas Carol*. But they can be irrelevant to your *own* futures if you pay attention to opportunities that open up for you. I want these lessons to be a playbook for you in how to make your way in this increasingly anonymous world. Because it's not the digital world that's going to make your life successful and easier. It's how you interact with people and how you win them over to your side.

Robots may take over in many ways. But they're never going to help you deal with an elderly parent, help you get your kids into Stanford or Notre Dame, or make love to you on your anniversary. We need real skin in the game, not something out of the 3-D printer. Make your lives as personal as you can; get yourself noticed in interesting ways. Be good to people and don't be afraid of teaching others certain tricks of the trade that you picked up from your own experiences.

This book began on New Year's Eve, and it's fitting that it ends on the same day four years later. We all make note of benchmarks, birthdays, and New Year's, natural moments where almost all of us look backward more than ahead. Resolutions never resonate as much as looking to the past, childhood, families both lost and still here, loves lost and gained, the good stuff, and the bad. And your youth.

This New Year's Eve I was at the apartment of a couple I have known since their engagement and marriage in 1963. I had worked as a counselor in a summer camp in Maine with the host, a man of common sense and knowledge about the foibles of human nature. Here's a typical pearl from him about relationships: "Wrong no man . . . and write no woman." Hmm . . . think about that. My friend is a lawyer and enjoys putting debatable concepts on the table. I believe in staying in touch with your past but not being dragged down by it. Preserve the friendships that can inspire or amuse you, and, as you give life lessons to others, know that sometimes those lessons can be turned around on you. One of the dinner guests this New Year's Eve was a brilliant one, a famous jurist at the highest state levels. I had recently gotten a phone call from one of her children, a bright young man who needed some help with a problem in his business. He left me a phone message. I called him back, got an answering machine, and told him, "Sure, call me at the office. But *never* on a Monday or before eleven in the morning."

One of my key lessons in life to young people is never to call anyone busy on a Monday morning for an interview or informational meeting. Or for a problem that's *not* part of the business of the person you're calling. Because it's only going to annoy the person who is starting his or her own business week. On Monday mornings he or she has more important things to do. The person will not be eager to talk to you again. It plants a bad seed, even a stupid one.

Well, the young man called me before 9 AM on the next Monday morning. I wasn't in. But when I arrived it annoyed me that he hadn't paid attention.

But because of my friendship with his mother, I did call him that Monday afternoon. And after I answered his question to me, I took the opportunity to tell him my practical rule of life about calling Monday mornings. He didn't skip a beat and said, "You know what *my* number one rule of life is?"

"No, what is it?" I answered.

"Always do what your mother tells you to do."

I laughed.

The judge and her husband drove me close to my home after the New Year's party. It was after 1 AM. The night was cold and the streets were deserted. We are not a late-night party town in wintry Boston.

But I kept laughing about the young man's response to me. I would hire someone like that if he were looking for a job. He separated himself from the crowd and gave me something precious, two things we can use every day: a different way of looking at the world. And a smile.

I'll leave *you* with hopes that every day of your young lives, you can find a belly laugh or two. It's the best therapy.

The Athenaeum
Saturday afternoon
January 3, 2015

ABOUT THE AUTHOR

John D. Spooner is one of the very few investment advisor/novelists in America. His best-selling nonfiction includes *Do You Want to Make Money or Would You Rather Fool Around?*, *Confessions of a Stockbroker*, *Smart People*, and *Sex and Money*. His novels include *Class* and *The Foursome*. His articles appear in magazines such as *Playboy, Town and Country,* the *Atlantic, Esquire, Time,* and the *Boston Globe.* His latest book, *No One Ever Told Us That: Money and Life Letters to My Grand-children,* has been a *Boston Globe* number one best seller, and number two on Amazon.com's best-selling business books list, and has been published in Korea, Japan, and China.

Spooner has been a director of the *Atlantic* and David R. Godine, Publisher, and has been a member of the Massachusetts Cultural Council, which distributes all arts funding for the Commonwealth of Massachusetts. He has been honored with the Literary Lights Award, bestowed on New England's most distinguished authors by the Boston Public Library.

A managing director for investments at a leading Wall Street firm, Spooner was also the creator of *A Book for Boston,* in honor of the city's three hundred fiftieth birthday. John lectures widely and has appeared on numerous television, radio, and Internet programs, including *Wall*

Street Week, CNBC, Fox News, and National Public Radio, on his philosophy of investing. He has been a frequent guest commentator on *Taking Stock* on Bloomberg Radio. Spooner was on the board of the Harvard Alumni Association and was cofounder of The Curious George Foundation. He now serves on the boards of the Boys and Girls Clubs, the Huntington Theatre, and WBUR.

Inc. magazine said about him, "Spooner, known nationally as the author of *Smart People* and *Confessions of a Stockbroker,* is a phenomenon, as much a psychologist and futurist as an investment advisor." The author Robert B. Parker has said that "Spooner is one of the best writers in America." Spooner has been a contributing editor of *Worth* magazine and business editor for *Boston* magazine. The *Improper Bostonian* magazine has voted him Boston's Best Investment Advisor. *Barron's* has named him one of the 100 Best Financial Advisors in America. The *Boston Globe* has referred to him as "a national treasure."

Spooner oversees assets for more than 800 families all over America and the world. A graduate of Harvard, John lives on Beacon Hill in Boston. For further information, e-mail him at spoonersmartpeople @earthlink.net, or go to his websites, johndspooner.com and nooneevertoldusthat.com, and webcast at TedxBeaconStreet/ johnspooner.

OTHER BOOKS BY
JOHN D. SPOONER

The Pheasant-lined Vest of Charlie Freeman, 1967
Three Cheers for War in General, 1968
Confessions of a Stockbroker, 1972
Class, 1973
The King of Terrors, 1975
Smart People, 1979
Sex and Money, 1985
A Book for Boston (creator), *1976*
The Foursome, 1993
*Do You Want to Make Money or Would You Rather Fool Around?,
    1999*
*No One Ever Told Us That: Money and Life Letters to My Grandchil-
    dren, 2012*

INDEX